For the Love of Scott!

by Jo Hamilton

Olmstead Publishing

2011 USA

For The Love of Scott!

By Jo Hamilton

ISBN13: 978-193419430-0

Formatting by Dr. Phyllis M Olmstead
Cover by KMS, Inc. Durham, NC

For permission contact the author at:
ForTheLoveOfScott23@gmail.com

Olmstead Publishing
www.olmsteadpublishing.com
apopka@usa.com

Jo Hamilton

Contents

Prologue 5
And It Begins in Iowa 7
The Wedding Day 15
The First Two Surprises 20
Here Comes Number Three 24
And Then There Were Four 29
Spot and Friends 32
Playing Doctor 35
Keep on Keeping On 38
Hang On, Jesus 41
And Then Came Number Five 43
Please Don't Lose My Baby Brother 47
Jumping Into Life 50
We Grew Up and Away 60
Get Your Game On 66
Let the Music Play 68
You Can Go Home 72
Mom, Please Make Me an Appointment 75
The Fight Begins 77
Let's Get This Party Started 84
Only Three More Months to Go 87
The Beginning of the Ninth 92
The Beginning of the End 95
You're Out! 105
The Death Vigil 116
The Last Christmas 123
Happy Birthday, Denny 130
Home, Where the Tall Corn Grows 138
The Other Scott 142
Afterward 144
What Can You Do to Stay Safe? 153
The Lessons Learned 165

For The Love of Scott!

Expressions of Gratitude.. 171
Author 173

Prologue

As my brother lay writhing in unimaginable pain, all he asked of me was, "You have to tell people what they did to me."

It was December 1983. Scott Hamilton, the Olympian, was fighting his way to his first Gold Medal in the Winter Olympics. The formidable figure skater was competing for the title in the Men's Single category. Scott had fought and won many battles in his young life already, beginning at two years of age when he was diagnosed with a mysterious illness.

Meanwhile, Scott Hamilton, my baby brother, already a gifted baseball player, was confronting an immense challenge of his own.

Scott, 2 years of age, 1962

These two exceptional men shared more than the same name. As you read

For The Love of Scott!

For the Love of Scott!, the uncanny parallels in their lives will astound you.

I promised my brother, Scott, that I would tell his story. I believe that I have one chance to get it right, as did the medical professionals who were entrusted with restoring his health.

It took decades for me to summon the strength to write this book. It meant revisiting painful and haunting images of the agonizing pain that my brother, Scott, was forced to endure in a medical center that prided itself on being "world class."

Could I forgive the condescending physicians and nurses who insisted that they were right and we were wrong? Their catastrophic medical errors changed the lives of our family forever.

Scott's spirit has long since moved on to a more enlightened world, yet I feel certain that he guided me in the writing of his story.

Jo Hamilton

And It Begins in Iowa

Scott was the fifth child born into our Irish-English Catholic family. We lived in a small rural farming community right smack in the middle of the USA, the part known as The Heartland of America, The Land Where the Tall Corn Grows, Heaven and Field of Dreams; in other words, Iowa.

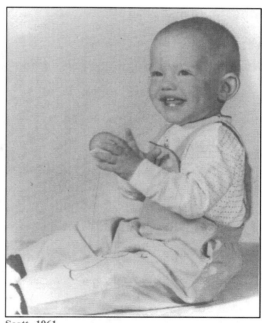

Scott--1961

For The Love of Scott!

I love my home state. Being from Iowa is about the best thing you could ever hope for. The dirt—oh how I *love* the dirt! It is so rich and black, especially after it rains. You open the window, suck in the air, and breathe, deeply.

For me, there is nothing that smells better in the whole world than that black soil.

As a young adult, I moved to the East Coast and soon decided to plant a small garden to reconnect with my farming roots. My Iowa family had a big laugh when I told them that I had to *buy* bags of black planting soil at the garden store to mix with the native red clay. There were not enough viable nutrients available in the Virginia dirt to sustain the vegetables that I wanted to grow in my garden.

Years later, when I was home for a Christmas visit, my youngest niece, Amy, and I went for a drive out to the family farm after dinner. I told her that I wanted to dig up some dirt, put it in a jar and take it back to Virginia with me so that, when I was homesick, I could just open the lid and take a big sniff. Amy was always up for any adventure and thought this was a great idea!

Armed with a Mason jar and a strong spoon, Amy and I headed to the farm. We dug and dug, slowly chipping away

8

at the frozen ground. It was a cold and windy winter day, only about 15 degrees.

Suddenly, the farmer who was renting the land from my father at the time showed up with his tractor. He hopped down from the seat and walked over to us. After introductions, I explained honestly to him that we were trying to dig up some dirt so that I could take it back East.

Amy added, "My Aunt Jo is homesick for Iowa dirt!"

The farmer did not bat an eye. He understood the nature of our mission and asked if we needed any help. We declined his kind offer and kept digging with Mom's bent tablespoon until we had filled the jar to about 3/4 full of the rich black soil.

It takes another Iowan to understand the importance of and the logic behind engaging in such a mission. Growing up in a small rural community in Iowa is like being in the TV show, *Little House on the Prairie*, every day. Where else do the people who pass you by in their car or pickup truck always wave? If you had car trouble or a roadside emergency, you did not have to wait more than 10 minutes for someone to stop and offer their help. No one needed AAA in Iowa!

For The Love of Scott!

Everyone in our town is connected, if not by blood, then by community. Whenever anyone needs help with something—lost livestock, a part for their combine, bringing in their crop, a ride or even a kidney—there was not a board or formal meeting required for the community to set up a plan to help a neighbor. Someone would make one phone call, then another and another. Within an hour or two, you had the part that was needed, a group of people to help, or someone to take you where you needed to go. This beautiful and simple system works because people care about each other and no one thinks about being reimbursed for their time or effort.

Our family lived on a farm about seven miles from town. The population was fewer than a thousand residents. Our entire school enrollment consisted of about 400 students including kindergarten through grade 12. Everyone knew everyone else, and the term, "it takes a village," accurately described our community. Whenever you did something good, everyone knew and celebrated with you. If you did something wrong, well, that became news as well!

Jo Hamilton

The kids in our town grew up feeling safe, secure and loved. It might be hard to believe but the bonds and connections that were made in this small, rural agricultural area have lasted a lifetime.

Recently, I went home for an all-school reunion. There, I talked with classmates who had planned their entire vacation around the event. The people who come back for the reunions every five years do so because, no matter what they have accomplished in life, where they live, or how much money they earn, small town rural Iowa remains the *only* place in August, on a reunion weekend!

For this very special and anticipated event, Main Street is closed off for a street dance. There is a parade. The local

Newell Providence School, Newell, Iowa

volunteer firefighters from surrounding towns challenge each other with ongoing water fights. You can tour the schoolhouse with your kids and grandkids, showing them where your formative years were spent. A lawn chair becomes the hottest commodity of the weekend!

As I walked into the formal banquet on Saturday night with my brothers, Denny and Mike, I felt the same kind of excitement that I had felt every year on the first day of school. The same questions filled my head, "Who would be there? Would they look the same? Would we remember and recognize each other? Would they seem different?" The time that I spent with old classmates and teachers was a direct transport back in time, stirring the feelings of days gone by. I would always fall in love with my hometown all over again.

There is nothing else in the world like this feeling. Hugs, kisses, email addresses and cell phone numbers are exchanged.

I do not really know what it is like growing up in another state. I do know that, when you are from Iowa and, you see an Iowa license plate on a vehicle driving through a parking lot anywhere, you follow the vehicle so you can talk to the driver and ask, "What part of Iowa are you from?"

Jo Hamilton

Once when I was shopping at a grocery store in Virginia, I was wearing my Iowa State University, hoodie and someone at the far end of the produce aisle yelled, "Are you from Iowa?"

I replied, "Yes."

They yelled back, "What part?"

This happens to me frequently, no matter where I might be.

Several years ago, I needed to have a breast lump removed and was referred to a surgeon who specialized in the procedure. I walked into her office nervous and anxious. My eyes immediately went to an embroidered framed picture of the state of Iowa hanging on the surgeon's wall. I was immediately at ease and knew that everything would be fine.

On the morning of my surgery, I saw my chart lying at the foot of my gurney. The very first line on the chart stated, "40-year-old white woman from Iowa." I laughed out loud! Every nurse in that pre-surgical unit now knew that I was from Iowa. My doctor made sure that her entire staff knew this fact because she, too, was from Iowa. One of the nurses told me, "This is one of the first things the doctor tells someone when she meets them. She is so proud of her roots." That is just the way we feel, proud to be an Iowan! Saying that there is a strong bond among Iowans is an understatement. Once fellow Iowans identify with one another, they become instant friends.

To this day, I am still in touch with that surgeon, and whenever I see her, the first thing we discuss is our home state of Iowa!

The Wedding Day

Our parents were kind, trusting, hardworking farmers who started their life together with little more than blind faith and their love for each other. Eddie and Lucy met at a dance hall in their hometown shortly after my father returned from World War II. He had been in the Navy, stationed in the Pacific on a ship, the LSM 232, after the attack on Pearl Harbor. Dad had just returned home and he was out on the town. My mom was also out partying that night with her best friend and three of her six sisters.

At the dance hall, a small group was standing around the jukebox talking when Mom and Dad each spotted a dime on the floor, at the same time. They both reached for it, bumping their heads. My dad used this as an opening to ask my mom to share the next dance.

And, so began their romance.

For The Love of Scott!

Eddie and Lucy were married on Friday, April 13, 1948. Some might question their choice of dates, especially after they were involved in an accident on the way home from the wedding ceremony! Their vehicle was rear-ended by a drunk driver whose car pushed theirs into and almost over an overpass bridge. Mom and Dad's car was teetering on the edge, preparing to fall nearly 50 feet onto the railroad tracks below! The damaged gas tank was leaking gasoline onto the rear seat and they were

Mr. and Mrs. Hamilton, April 13, 1948

still inside! Fortunately, for them, a friendly farmer on his tractor, came by and helped pull the vehicle back from the edge before it could plunge over the rail. Truly, Mom and Dad had a wedding day to remember!

Their first farmland was a rental property that had been

Mom and Dad, August 1963

condemned. It was so full of weeds and cockleburs that no one else wanted to farm it.

In those early years, my parents crawled on their hands and knees through the rows of corn and beans, pulling the weeds by hand because they were too thick to be removed any other way.

Mom and Dad had deep faith, strong backs, and genuine hope that they could turn the land into a

sustainable and profitable family farm. For a little extra cash, they also maintained a country school located on the farm. They bought laying chickens and some livestock. Little by little, Mom and Dad built their lives and a family together.

One day a few months after the wedding, Mom and Dad were making a trip to the local dump to haul away some dead trees and brush that they had cleared from the farm. Shortly after arriving, Mom heard a weak whimpering sound and found a frightened, very dirty, very young mixed Collie puppy buried in the refuse. She

immediately claimed the puppy. She and my father put him in their truck, took him home and

Mom, Denny, Jo, and Lucky, enjoying a sunny day on the farm!

promptly named him, Lucky. What a wise decision! My parents could not have known then what a major part Lucky would play in their lives and the lives of their unborn children.

My dad was an avid athlete. He *loved* baseball. Because he could not afford a car when he was younger, Dad would walk seven miles to and from town to practice with the high school team after school. Later on, he bought a small motor scooter that became his "dream machine." The scooter was big enough to hold Dad's books and equipment and, even, his little dog, Spot, whenever he wanted to ride along.

Dad was a talented third baseman. After his high school graduation, my father continued to hone his skills and went on to play semipro baseball. Dad's passion for baseball was so great that he hoped at least of his children who would share his dedication to the game. My father's wish would eventually be granted. All of his children were good athletes, especially his youngest son, Scott, who turned out to be a stellar baseball player. Scott also inherited Dad's resilience and powerful determination.

Dad and Spot--1940

As a very small child, I remember how my mother would pack snacks and drinks on Sunday afternoons after church and then, take my oldest brother and me to watch my Dad play ball. On some days, there would be two or three games, which meant that we were at the field for the entire day.

For The Love of Scott!

Once, a line drive smacked Dad right in the mouth, knocking out a couple of his teeth. It was all very bloody and scary for two youngsters. Despite his injury, my Dad did not leave the game. He did not even cry.

The First Two Surprises

Eddie and Lucy's first children came as a duet within the first year of their marriage. The twins, Dennis Linn and Deanna Lynn were born two months premature and had respiratory problems.

It was December 30, 1948, in the middle of a brutal and long winter. The hospital was crowded with other war baby births, so the twins were taken to the nursery and placed in dresser drawers for a few days. My mother needed to recover and become strong enough to take the twins home with her.

I have heard this story told by my parents many times over the years. As my dad waited outside the delivery room for the birth of his first born, a nurse brought my baby sister to him wrapped in a pink blanket. She said, "Congratulations, you have a girl!"

My Dad was excited and relieved.

A few minutes later, another nurse came out with another baby and said, "And, a boy."

In a state of disbelief and shock, my Dad said, "Is that one mine, too?" When the nurse answered "Yes," he passed out, hitting the hard tiled floor!

Back then, there were no sonograms available for determining the gender of an unborn baby or even the quantity—so everyone, including the doctor, was surprised by the twins' arrival!

Later complications ensued from the delivery. Mom was readmitted to the hospital for a few more days, leaving

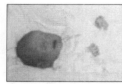
Deanna Hamilton--1949

Dad home alone with two newborns. A couple nearby neighbors came over to help him with feedings and diaper changes until our Mom came back home. Somehow, Dad and the twins survived.

For a few weeks things seemed to be okay, but as is often the case with premature births, the babies' small lungs were slow to develop. Both Denny and Deanna came down with pneumonia. It went downhill from there.

What should have been a joyful celebration in the month of her birth instead became a sad one, ending with her death. On the 23rd day of February, 1949, Deanna Lynn went to heaven. The medical personnel placed her little body in a shoebox and my aunt and uncle drove her to the funeral home.

Deanna looked so beautiful wearing a long, white baby gown in the only photo of I ever saw of her. She had a full head of black hair. It was proof enough that she had lived and that I did have a sister.

That was the first catastrophic event that occurred between the medical profession and my family. The premature newborns had compromised respiratory systems. At the very minimum Denny and Deanna should have been given oxygen and placed into incubators. Their beds should have been tilted to allow proper fluid drainage from their underdeveloped lungs. Instead, they were placed into dresser drawers.

Codeine cough syrup had been prescribed for Deanna and the twins had been dismissed from the hospital during a horrendous winter storm season. Our parents managed weekly trips with the babies back and forth to the hospital during the next month for their checkups. Doctors continued to keep Deanna on the codeine even though she kept losing weight and her cough worsened. The day she died, Deanna had vomited up volumes of the cough medicine and could barely breathe. Neglect, incompetence, fate—whatever it was, she was gone.

A few weeks later, Tetracycline was approved and became available. It was too late for little Deanna but the antibiotic was given to Denny and it saved his life.

Here Comes Number Three

I was born the following March. The year was 1950.

For a long time, I had wondered how it made my parents feel to have another girl so soon after the passing of my sister. Was I a constant reminder of the sad past? Were they happy at the promise of an exciting future for this new life? My guess is that it was both.

I often imagined what life would have been like if my sister had lived. Would she have liked sports? Would she have looked like me? Would we have been best friends? Would she have liked housework? I was given the name, Jo, after the character, Jo March, in the book, *Little Women*. The priest of our parish at the time told my parents that "Jo" was not considered an authentic Christian name and could not be used on my baptismal certificate. Within minutes, I became Josephine. It didn't matter. As soon as I could, I changed the name back again and Jo became my permanent label. I was never really a Josephine!

My start in life turned out to be another medical challenge for my parents. At some point during my

Jo Hamilton

embryonic development, the opening between my esophagus and stomach was not completely formed thus making it impossible to get nutrition into my newborn body. I barely weighed five pounds at birth and started losing weight immediately. I dropped to under four pounds. The doctors said I was too small and weak for surgery. Time was running out.

My parents prayed for a miracle. Their appeal was

answered by a medical team in a larger city. The doctors used some special kind of prescription drops to dissolve the thin membrane that was causing the blockage and, here I am today.

Jo and Denny 3 and 4 years old

Living proof, that on a good day, medicine is a wonderful marvel!

Because Denny and I were so close in age and because we were the only two siblings at the time, we became inseparable. Our cribs were set up facing each other in the nursery. Whether we were taking our afternoon naps or going to bed for the night, Denny's face was the last one I would see before I closed my eyes. I watched intently as he learned to climb out of his baby bed. From then on, I was always just one-step behind him, trying to keep up.

I loved having a big brother all to myself, and Denny was the best. Laid back and calm, he would let me boss him around to my heart's content.

One day in the fall, five-year-old Denny and I, at age 4, were playing outside. Dad was on his tractor getting ready to head out into the plowed field to spread a load of manure that he had cleaned out from the pigpen. He had just turned the boar, a large adult male pig, out into the pig lot with several fertile sows. Dad was trying to breed them so that he could get his feeder pig business started. He stopped at the gate and told Denny and me NOT to climb over the fence and into the pigpen because the ill-tempered boar might hurt us.

As soon as Dad was out of sight, Denny decided that he was not afraid of any old boar. Up and over the fence he went. I kept telling him to come back, but Denny would not listen to me. "Adventure-Boy "was too distracted while climbing on the cob pile to notice that the boar was running from the far side of the pig lot and heading right towards him.

Jo Hamilton

Mom must have been watching out the kitchen window because, about the same time the boar grabbed Denny in his jaws, she ran out of the house screaming at the top of her lungs at the boar, "Stop, stop, put him down!"

I was crying. The boar had taken off running with my brother between his jaws. Denny was bouncing up and

down, his head and legs flailing in all directions. He was crying and screaming, scared out of his mind!

Then, out of nowhere came Lucky, running at full throttle. Lucky hit the boar full force in the rear, chomping down on the rear

Denny, Lucky, and Jo, summer 1955

end of the boars' most vulnerable parts and hanging on for dear life!

The boar immediately spun around to see what the heck had attached itself to his bacon and, in doing so, opened his jaws. Denny went sailing up into the air, landing on the cob pile.

Lucky continued to chase the boar down into the pasture, far away from all of us.

Mom was there in a heartbeat, gathering Denny up and checking him over. The boar's teeth had bitten through Denny's clothes, leaving deep marks on his skin, but there were no life-threatening injuries.

The doctor checked Denny over and, except for some bruising, cuts, and sore muscles; he was as good as new in a very short time. Lucky got to sleep in the house that night instead of the barn and, instead of the usual table scraps; he had a big steak for dinner. His place in the family had been elevated forever. We all knew then that it had been no accident when Lucky found my parents at the dump that day. *We* were the lucky ones!

Lucky continued to show his love and gratitude to us in many ways as he lived out his long life with our family on the farm.

Jo Hamilton

And Then There Were Four

When I was five years old, my parents told us we were going to have a new baby. This was the best news ever! I had been secretly praying a long time for a baby sister and finally, my dream was going to come true.

Mike hopeful ball player, 1956

I still remember the day that my mother said to me, "We are going to have a new baby!" It was summertime and we were upstairs in one of the storage rooms, cleaning it out. My mother loved to clean. We had no inside plumbing and no indoor bathroom but I would put up any amount of money to prove that we had the cleanest house within 25 miles. I had endless debates with my mother about why we had to repeatedly do the same house cleaning work, claiming it was a waste of time and was not improving our minds one bit. She would always assure me that the cleaning was not really the point. Mom would say, "There are other lessons for you to learn that have nothing to do with your brain."

I do not remember ever feeling as if we were poor or deprived even though we were probably the only family in our area that had to go outside to use the bathroom, or hand pump and heat water to bathe in or wash our dishes and

clothes. My brothers and I did not know any different and we did not care. We were always clean and never hungry.

Lassie, Mike, Jo, Mom, and Denny feeding a baby rabbit

To me, it was like living a modern day version of *Lassie*! We had acres and acres to play on, with fields of grass, tall trees and animals to love and care for. We had the sky, the creek and the dirt. In the summer, my brothers and I spent hours on our backs lying on the grass, looking up at the clouds and making up some very impressive

Jo Hamilton

stories. We had a big garden to tend with lots of vegetables and watermelon. We would play "farm" with our little plastic tractors and cars. We would run through the fields of sweet corn playing hide and seek for hours. We had books and our imaginations and most of all, we had each other. Life was fun and so very good.

Now it was going to get even better because I might be getting a baby sister! Yeah!

Denny and I were asked to help my mother more around the house and to be on extra special behavior so she would not get upset with us. I can assure you that we really were great little kids. I think my parents just wanted to make sure that their kids would not start acting up now that a third little person was on the way.

When the day of the event arrived, September 29, 1955, Denny and I went to stay with an aunt and uncle until our mom and dad brought little Michael Edward home from the hospital. He was so beautiful.

To this day, my mother will tell you that Mike was the best and healthiest baby she ever had. This has remained true throughout his entire life, even when Mike grew into adolescence and adulthood. He was kind, sweet, talented, handsome, smart, and a gifted athlete. Except for his flat feet, Mike was the healthiest of all her newborns.

Mike was a great little brother. He would play house with me without complaint, playing as if he was the neighbor, my child, or whatever role our little imaginations could dream up. More importantly, Mike was my friend, my special buddy. We loved our lives, playing away the time while living on our farm.

Spot and Friends

My brothers and I named all of our farm animals: sheep, pigs, cows, rabbits and chickens, kittens and dogs. One of our pigs was named Spot. She was a 150-pound sow, female pig, which was all white with a large black spot on her left side. I loved that pig! I would coax Spot over to the fence with a big ear of corn and then climb onto her back. She would carry me all around the pasture. I trained her to turn left if I scratched her left ear with my left foot, or right if I scratched her right ear with my right foot. If I said, "Whoa," Spot would stop completely.

On hot summer days, she loved to find the biggest mud hole in the pasture. She would slowly make her way over to the hole, grunting softly as she walked with me still on her back, riding along. Grunting was her way of warning me to get off NOW if I did not want to go into the muddy water hole with her. Of course, there was a learning curve involved and I did not realize the first time exactly what was happening until it was too late. She walked into the hole until the muddy water was up to her belly, which meant that it was above my knees. Then down she went-- ker-plop!

We both got cooled off, however, HER Mother did not yell at her and ask, "Do you know how dirty you are? What happened? How are your clothes EVER going to be clean again?" I did not care that my mother was so upset. Getting dirty was worth it! I looked like I had just been dipped in dark chocolate! Spot must have liked it too because she tried to take me to that mud hole many more times.

Anyone who thinks pigs are dumb has never been around them for very long. Spot was gentle and sweet and, since I did not have a horse, she was the best ride that I had.

One summer day when I went out to the fence to take a ride, I could not find Spot anywhere. I called and called for her but, she never appeared. I ran crying to the house.

For The Love of Scott!

Mom could not explain where my pet was but, when my dad came up from the field, he told me, "Spot went to the market," whatever that meant. It must have satisfied me because I do not remember worrying about her after that. In my little girl's mind, Spot was on an adventure.

Little did I know then that the bacon my family and I would be consuming over the next few months was compliments of Spot, the best feeder pig we had on the farm. Not a fair price to pay for coming in first!

Jo Hamilton

Playing Doctor

Our parents sacrificed a farm animal to feed our family when necessary yet, they taught us kindness and reverence for all things living. They taught us how to identify different grasses, flowers and trees, the reasons that we rotated crops in the fields and ways to read the sky. We knew the difference between the bad storm clouds and tornado clouds. I watched my father operate on sick and injured critters and deliver newborn baby animals. He fixed broken machinery and worked spreadsheets. Dad could calculate feed for livestock, seed for planting, and the best formula for fertilizer. He could remodel a room or build a whole new building. Like most farmers, our dad could have invented the term "multitasking"!

One summer day, when I was six years old, my father had to go over to a neighbor's farm and help them bring in their hay crop. He had a very pregnant sow, that was about to farrow or give birth. Dad asked me to keep an eye on her in case she delivered before he returned. He had already placed her inside the hog house in a pen with a bed of straw.

To me that translated to, "You are in charge of birthing these piglets."

The minute my dad left, I ran to the house and raided my mother's kitchen. I knew exactly what to get, grabbing dishtowels and rags that were soft and clean, and necessary for a successful delivery of those babies. I did not have a mask so I used a brown paper bag and cut holes out for my eyes. I then took Mom's Playtex® Living® Gloves from under the sink. They were about five sizes too big, but also very necessary for the task that I was about to complete.

Climbing into the pigpen, I sat in a corner with the bag over my head and those big gloves waving back and forth on my small hands—all in 90-degree heat! I listened silently as the mother pig grunted and groaned, preparing to give birth. It took hours but I was too excited to care about the heat or the danger. Sows can be very mean and aggressive when they are about to give birth.

Suddenly, the sow raised her head and let out a loud grunt. Out popped a pink, slimy baby pig!

Jo Hamilton

I slowly crawled over to the sow on my hands and knees to where the baby piglet lay. Gently picking up the tiny, still being, I placed it in my mom's clean white dishtowel and gently began to rub off the sticky slime. I was very careful to clean the piglet's mouth first and remove the birth sac around its nose just as I had seen my dad do on many occasions. I worked my way backwards, cleaning and rubbing every inch of that baby pig's body until it was clean as a whistle and dry as a bone. Then, I carefully placed the piglet next to the mom's belly so it could begin its first meal.

Within seconds, another piglet was born. I have no way of knowing exactly how long the entire delivery process lasted but, when the sow was done, we had delivered 14 piglets who were all safe and sound, nursing frantically at their mother's table.

Still sitting in the pigpen admiring the new family and feeling very content, I heard my fathers' voice say, "Looks like I left my sow in good hands today." He seemed amused yet serious.

My mother did not share Dad's amusement, however. She had an old crank-pulley clothes washer full of dirty

towels and rags that I had delivered to her along with those
Playtex® Living® Gloves. Mom immediately deposited
the gloves into the trash!

Keep on Keeping On

Our parents were successfully managing both a family
and a farm business that was productive and profitable.

For the next five years, life was seamless. My parents
bought their first farm. We now had our own roots.
Everyone sighed as our family relaxed into a rhythm of a
life that was simple, rich and full of hard, honest work. As
anyone that grew up on a farm knows, the chores are
endless, especially if you have livestock. You never take a
vacation. You always have plenty to do because the work is
literally never done.

The winters were especially harsh in the Midwest. They
could last for four or five months. When the spring thaw
finally came, we battened down the hatches and prepared
for the tornados! It all seemed like a great adventure to me,
as a young child.

In the winter, Mom would spend several minutes on
each of us kids daily. She helped us put on coats, boots,

hats, gloves, scarves and mittens so that we could go out in
the snow and make a fort, dig a tunnel or go sledding, only
to have us come back into the house within a few hours,
soaked to the skin and freezing. We would make a mess of
her polished hard wood floors, flinging wet clothes in every
direction. Denny, Mike and I would be laughing and
giggling, full of excitement about all the wonders we had
shared that day in our winter wonderland, as we gathered
inside around the warm, oil-burning stove.

When the temperatures would drop below freezing, as it
did most of the winter, we would take turns going out to
stoke and rekindle the fire in the water tank heater. It was a
long, enclosed, hollow steel shaft that would be placed in
the cattle's water tank during the winter months. Ideally,
the tank heater would get hot enough to keep the water in
the tank from freezing.

We were all fascinated with the fire and spent hours
standing by the tank heater putting corncobs, coal, and
wood into it to keep it burning around the clock. If the tank
heater was kept at a high enough temperature, it prevented
the drinking water in the livestock's water tank from
freezing. If the fire went out, the three-foot deep tank

would freeze solid in the water and would not thaw out again until spring. That meant you would be carrying five-gallon buckets of water all day, every day and night to the milk cows, pigs, and cattle so they would have fresh drinking water. The fire in the heater went out only once during those long, cold winters and it never happened again! We had a great team system worked out and, once perfected, it worked like a fine tuned machine!

There were many life lessons to be learned from farm life, some harder than others. It was such great preparation for our adult lives. One of the best lessons of all was how we would all work together to accomplish something that needed to be done. No excuses! No crying! And, no whining! We were told what had to be done, we made a plan, and we just did it.

Hang On, Jesus

Denny, Mike, and I had vivid imaginations and, at every opportunity, we used them to the fullest. I remember in particular one Easter Sunday at church. My family was sitting in a pew about half way up to the front altar.

During the service, I started getting antsy. Mom gave me her rosary to play with in order to keep me quiet. I studied it and counted the beads over and over again. The hand-carved crucifix that hung at the end of the beads fascinated me. I decided to twirl that rosary round and round and round over my head like a lasso, using the cross for the handle. It was making quite an interesting whirring sound as it went around faster and faster.

People were preparing for communion, their heads bowed in prayer. The silence in the church was profound.

Suddenly, I exclaimed in a loud voice, "Hang on, Jesus, you're going for a ride!" and then, I let the rosary fly right out of my hand and up toward the communion rail.

Although my mother was probably laughing on the inside, she appeared horrified on the outside. She leaned over to me and said, "March right up there and retrieve that rosary!"

That was not a problem for me. It had been my desire all along to get out of that seat and go somewhere!

As I was returning to our pew, rosary in hand, I noticed that quite a few people were grinning and snickering at me. I smiled back. It was wonderful to see so many happy people in church on that special Easter Sunday!

And Then Came Number Five

Life and time flew by on the farm. Another five years passed. I guess my parents thought that, maybe, one more time would be the charm, or perhaps, it was the diaper bag mistakenly left at our house by one of my mother's seven sisters. The diaper bag had quite a history. In the past, every time one of my mother's sisters had accidentally left the diaper bag at one of their sibling's house, that sister would end up pregnant.

This is exactly what happened to our mom. One of our aunts left her diaper bag and, the next thing we knew, our mother was the pregnant one. We were going to have another new baby!

I was now ten, a little older and a lot wiser, so I started negotiating with my mom as to why this baby had to be a girl, no excuses or mistakes. "Mom, when you go to the hospital, would you make sure you pick up a girl this time, please?"

I was not having any trouble with my two brothers. Life with them was easy, breezy. I just told them what to do and they did it. Mike would play house, dolls, or farm with me whenever I asked. Denny and I would go fishing or ride our homemade motor scooters together whenever we had some free time. The biggest problem was that neither of them helped me with the housework or cleaning. They got to be outside with Dad and our animals, doing all the fun things.

Whenever I was given the choice of inside house cleaning or cleaning out the hog house, chicken house or barn, I would pick anything outside, even if it involved manure. Hey, I was a farm girl through and through and, to me, that meant being outside farming.

So, after a few months of waiting, one morning when we came down the stairs, the suitcase under the bed was missing. It was September 22, 1960.

Off to school the three of us went to await the news. It was late in the morning when I was called into the office through the school's intercom system. Walking to the office, I spotted my oldest brother, Denny, coming down the hallway towards me. We both knew that our lives were about to change forever and we were very excited.

Mike was in the kindergarten class in another part of the building. He would not find out the news until we saw him on the school bus later in the day.

We had a wonderful secretary at our school that was in charge of everything. Helen had known our dad when he went to this school many years earlier. She was the guardian of it all, K through 12. Helen had a long history at our school. She knew all the kids by name as well as their parents and, probably, their grandparents, too.

Helen asked Denny and me to sit down and explained that my Dad had called, asking her to tell us that we had a new baby. . . brother!

I was dumbfounded. How could this be? It must be a huge mistake. I clearly remember looking at Helen and shaking my head saying, "Not another brother, not another brother. It has to be a mistake! It has to be! Are you sure he said brother?"

She assured me that my dad had clearly said the word, brother, and that I should be happy because he was healthy and my mom was okay.

Denny looked at me and said, "This is the best thing ever. I have another brother."

I am sure that I glared at him in disgust. When we left the office, Denny was practically skipping and I was fighting back tears. "How could my mother do this to me again? I was so outnumbered, it just wasn't fair," I thought.

That night around the supper table, we all voted on what to name this new little boy. After eliminating Brad and Sean, he was to be christened Scott Alan Hamilton.

I had desperately wanted a sister but once we got past the sibling rivalry stage, I would eventually realize that having Scott as a brother was like hitting the lottery. I also came to understand that having three brothers meant that I had three faithful companions, protectors, allies and forever friends. There was never a day that I wished it were different. I never had to share a room or a dress yet, I always got to drive their cars and ride their motorcycles.

My brothers helped me to become a competitive athlete and a much better person.

Please Don't Lose My Baby Brother

The next day was Saturday so my dad took us to the hospital to visit our mom. There were very strict rules at the hospital and we were all too young to be allowed in her room. Instead, Mom stood at her window on the fourth floor. We waved to her from ground level, crying our eyes out, missing her beyond measure. We just wanted our mom to come home so that we could be a family again.

But, this was not meant to be just yet. Mother came down with pneumonia so she was not able to come home for several days. When she finally did, Scott would not be with her because she was still too weak to care for him. I worried constantly that someone might take our baby by mistake or that Mom would change her mind and decide to leave him there permanently.

A few days later, though, our mom finally told us that, when we came home from school, Scott would be there.

That day seemed to last forever but the wait was finally over. When we arrived at home, got off the bus, and ran into the house, there he was in the tiny bassinet sound

asleep. Scott was so small but he looked amazing! I had a
baby brother and felt like he was mine, all mine.

I know that my mom gave birth to Scott, but I was
convinced she had done it for me and only me. I was finally
getting to meet our newest family member. Our fates were
sealed in the heavens and I whispered to him that I would
take care of him for the rest of his life! Besides, I figured
Mom owed me, after mixing up the genders! I could not
wait to hold him. My parents were not as confident that I
was ready for this. They invented ways for me to prop him
up in order for me to hold him on my lap or in the rocking
chair yet, still have a feeling of being independent.

Scott developed an allergy to milk. He suffered from
colic for many months until they were able to find a
formula that he could tolerate. Because of this, I became his
designated rocker. He was hungry all the time yet, every
time he would eat, his little legs would draw up to his
small, empty belly, screaming in pain. There was little that
would console him. For some unknown reason, when I
would hold and rock Scott in my Grandma's old rocking
chair and talk or sing to him, he would calm down and fall
asleep.

Jo Hamilton

To this day, I have a special place in my heart for soybeans because soybean milk gave my baby brother his chance at life. Sobee™ was the only milk that Scott was able to digest. Almost overnight, he started to thrive.

Scott tried with all his might to keep up with the three of us. He learned to throw a baseball fast and straight, long before his little fingers could even hold it tight. He could swing and hit the ball if you could get it even remotely close to the plate. Our dad was so proud of Scott!

When it came to basketball, Scott quickly learned to dribble by bouncing the basketball again and again, hours at a time. He would try to make a basket by jumping and shooting, over and over. The basketball would go only halfway up to the rim yet, he was never discouraged. Scott

Baby Scott, me, Mike, and Denny, 1960

kept practicing the same shot repeatedly, just as he had watched us do many times before. His misses did not matter to Scott as long as he was with his brothers and sister doing the same thing that they were doing, being part of the team.

Jumping Into Life

When little Scottie was about three or four years old, we were all up in the hayloft playing. Scott had just learned how to climb the vertical ladder that led to the upper level. As had often happened, Denny, Mike, and I got bored once we had located the batch of kittens behind several bales of hay. It was the third time in a week that we had located the same litter. The mother cat would no doubt be moving them again that day, trying to keep one-step ahead of us.

Denny, Mike, and I took off, jumping down through the opening in which one would normally throw the bales of hay used for feeding the livestock. It was a soft landing below onto several layers of straw on the barn floor. Once we hit the ground, Mike and I took off out of the barn on the run. We left Scott alone, to fend for himself in getting down from the loft, not even worrying if he could navigate the ladder.

Coming down the ladder could be a lot scarier than going up especially if it was your first time and there was no one there to guide you. Little Scottie had no choice since we had already left.

It was not until we heard Scott crying as he came around the corner of the corncrib that we realized how thoughtless we had been. When backing down the ladder, Scott slipped and fell through the lower bottom of the barn door and onto the cement slab outside the door.

Blood was streaming down the side of his head! I yelled at Mom to come quick while I ran into the house to get some clean rags and bandages. Once Mom examined Scott's head wound, she knew it was too deep to heal on its own.

The local fire department and ambulance service consisted of local volunteers who dedicated their free time for training and responding to emergency calls. They came from nearby local farms or other communities close by and many drove on gravel roads in all kinds of weather to reach the Fire House in town. Once everyone had arrived, they would load up the rigs and take off to wherever the emergency might be. On that day, it was quicker to drive Scott into town ourselves. Mom drove the car while I cradled Scott on my lap and tried to comfort him during the seven long miles to the doctor's office.

We were fortunate to have a great doctor in our tiny little town. Doc could do everything. He could adjust your back or neck, take x-rays, prescribe medicine, or set your broken finger, ankle or arm. He could stitch you up and explain a serious condition to you with the compassion of a friend. Having Doc was a luxury most small towns did not experience. It was a true blessing because the closest hospital was several miles away.

Scotty was so brave. When Doc stuck the needle under his skin to numb him up, he never cried. As the doctor began to stitch up his head, we all breathed easier.

Scott looked up at the doctor and said in a very serious little voice, "You might as well sew up my pants while you're at it!" It

Scott resting after his visit to the doctor's office

52

Jo Hamilton

seemed that during the fall he had ripped a hole in one of his pant legs. It made total sense to Scott that his pants could be fixed right along with his head, saving our mom some extra work and time. Scottie was always thinking of others, even at his young age.

One hot summer day on the farm, Mike, Scott and I were really bored. We had finished all our chores and had some free time to go have fun. I was about thirteen years old at the time. Mike was about eight and Scott was just barely old enough to run around, trying to keep up with us. In the sixties, everyone smoked cigarettes (and other things!). You saw ads on television and in the movies. It could be fascinating to watch, as the smokers would deeply draw smoke into their lungs, hold it and then exhale. Sometimes the smoke would circle around their heads and back through their mouths. Some people would even pull it into and through their noses. It looked like magic and seemed like a really cool, grown up thing to do.

I suggested to Mike that we should try it and he agreed. Of course, we did not have any cigarettes and because of our geographic location, we did not have access to any. Once again, we had to call upon our imaginations to invent some. I sent Mike into the house for some stick matches, which were readily available to us. We used them to burn the trash once a week. We had a large empty barrel placed in a small, open clearing far away from everything. It was in this area we would take anything that would burn and fire it up. Of the four kids, only Denny and I were allowed to burn trash—Mike was still too little. He and Scott would watch the fire from a safe distance. To us it was like "a rite of passage" to be trusted with matches!

The three of us were standing in the shaded alleyway of the corncrib. There was a nice cool breeze blowing through. It was then I spotted an old corn stalk. It was the perfect length and width. I asked Scott for a match and told Mike I would get it started and then he could try it. Well after a long minute, all we had was a little smoke and no ignition. I sucked on that cornstalk with all my might and nothing! Mike thought it might start easier if I wrapped some of the brown silk around it at the end.

Great idea! I had seen Dad use the dry silk to start other fires and knew it would work. So, I found some brown silk that was nice and dry and wrapped it around the end of the small corn stalk several times. Scott gave me another

Jo Hamilton

match. They both stood there wide-eyed in anticipation of what would happen next.

I struck the match on the cement floor and put it up to the end of the cornstalk. At the same time, I took a really deep breath to get it going, and then came the breeze, blowing through the alleyway I heard crackling; I saw smoke and immediately smelled something burning. My lips were burning, my bangs and eyebrows were burnt, and I was spitting and coughing and yelling, "Ow! Oww! Owwww!!"

Mike and Scott were horrified. I was more worried about how I was going to explain my toasted lips, singed bangs and eyebrows, than the fact that I could not breathe. Obviously, there was more to this smoking thing than we knew! It was the last time we ever thought about smoking a corn stalk or anything else. The one good thing about our misadventures was I never had to worry about Mike or Scott ratting us out—no matter what the outcome. We always had each other's back.

As hard as we worked, we had equally as much fun, if not more. My Dad passed along his love for motorcycles to each one of us kids. Thanks to my father, before we had bicycles, we had homemade motor scooters. Denny's was red and mine was blue. They had old Briggs and Stratton™ lawn mower engines mounted on welded homemade frames. Denny and I designed a track in the front yard and raced around and around it trying to beat each other by the end of the designated laps. There would be dust flying everywhere. We would look like baby raccoons when we would come in from that dusty race. I remember my mom taking a wash cloth to our ears and necks and telling us she would never get it clean again! We knew between the Tide® and the Clorox® it would "all come out in the wash"! I have to say, it did not deter us one bit from doing it again the next day! Poor Mom! Of course, over time, we got bored doing the same old thing, so eventually we started building ramps with old cinder blocks and wooden boards. The next challenge was to see how high and how far we could jump those mighty scooters!! That was GREAT fun!

One day we decided to step it up a notch. We were told we could NOT ride the scooters on the public gravel road in front of our house. So, we decided to race down the ditches on either side of the road. We would each pick a parallel ditch for ourselves. Mike or Scott would yell, "Go" and away we went, racing as fast as those scooters would travel! Mike or Scott would be at the finish line to declare the winner. This entertained us for quite a while, but again the challenge eventually decreased and we were forced to come up with a new and more adventurous idea.

I think it was Denny who thought it would be really cool to set up a ramp and jump the scooters OVER the road. Technically, we would not be riding ON the road if we were in mid-air at the time we cleared the road. I thought it was a brilliant idea. So, we moved the cinder blocks and boards down the driveway into the widest part of the ditch and set up our new ramps.

It took several trial and error attempts, to get everything set just right so we could actually clear the road which was about ten-foot across, and land safely on the other side. Finally, we perfected our techniques and began jumping. First, we did it one at a time. One of us would watch, while the other one jumped. When that became too easy, we decided to jump simultaneously. I only wish one of my little brothers had been videotaping our stunts. I am sure we looked awesome! It didn't take long for us to realize we could do one better.

For The Love of Scott!

There wasn't a lot of traffic on our gravel road, if you didn't count the tractors and trailers. Once in a while a neighbor would go by in their car or pick up on their way to town for an errand. At some point, we decided it would be fantastic if Denny and I would shoot out of the ditch at the same time and jump across the road, on our scooters, right in front of a car!

What could possibly go wrong with THAT plan? As is the case with youth, we didn't think beyond the initial excitement of it. So, Mike and Scott were our "scouts," as Denny and I lay in wait, at the bottom of the steep ditch. We were opposite each other, hiding in the tall grass, revving our engines, hyped with adrenaline.

Somebody yelled, "Here comes a car, here comes a car!" It was our neighbor, Zora. Zora and Glen lived about two miles from us down a long dirt road. Zora was not a speed demon by any sense of the word and it could take a while for her to get to the point of execution. We depended heavily on Mike and Scott to be accurate with their decision in telling us when to jump, because we were too far down in the ditch to see anything but the crest of the road.

Jo Hamilton

Finally, we heard the signal and we blasted off. It was a perfect launch. While Zora was busy waving to Mike and Scott who were standing at the end of our lane by the mailbox, Denny and I went flying across the road directly in front of Zora's car! She hit her brakes and swerved. I am sure she had no idea what she had just witnessed, but she ended up in the ditch. She was not hurt but she was clearly shaken up.

Before we could even fully begin to enjoy the thrill of what we had just accomplished, we had to go get our Dad and his tractor and help pull Zora out of the ditch. We apologized to her and my parents apologized to her. Our scooters were put in indefinite storage under lock and key. It was rough on all four of us. Looking back on that day, I still get all tingly just thinking about it. It was exciting, it was fun, it was dangerous and it was extremely stupid. I am now convinced more than ever, my siblings and I must have had some very tired guardian angels working overtime on our behalves!!

We Grew Up and Away

Denny and Dad--1967

His entire life, Denny was small for his age. He never really grew into his own body until he came back from Navy boot camp during the Viet Nam war, bigger than our dad! This photo of our dad and him standing side by side says it all. Both are looking very handsome and proud in their Navy uniforms, grinning from ear to ear.

It was 1967. Our country was at war in Viet Nam. It was also a time of great controversy even in our small little community.

Fathers were trying desperately to get doctors to write letters in order to keep their sons home. Everyone was worried. The draft was reinstated and the draftees were selected by a government lottery system. Someone from the Department of Defense would draw a number and attach it to a letter of the alphabet. They would match that letter to the first letter of your last name and attach it to the number. That number would decide how quickly you would be drafted into the military.

My brother, Denny, and his best friend decided not to risk the lottery. They volunteered and took early enlistment while they were still seniors in high school.

Dad had many conversations with my brother, his friend, his friends' parents, and our mom. Together, they decided that the Navy was the safer route to go. None of us liked the odds or agreed with the war but, since my dad was a Navy vet, he was very patriotic and felt that the experience would be a good one for his oldest son. Denny would see some of the world and get an education when he came home.

Influenced in part by my dad, the two young men chose the Navy as the branch of service in which they wanted to serve.

It was at this point that our parents announced to us that we were going to take a family vacation before Denny was to leave. We would be taking the Union Pacific train all the way to the west coast and back, stopping off in Las Vegas to visit our aunt and uncle and their family.

I was a junior in high school and the last thing I wanted to do was spend three weeks of my summer away from home. What about my boyfriend, my girlfriends? I would miss so much in the social arena in two weeks' time, so much, that I would never catch up. I suppose I was just a typical narcissistic teenager.

That trip turned out to be one of the best times we had as a family and the last time we were all together for an extended family vacation. We saw so much of our country. For kids who had never been off the farm except for a few fishing trips to Minnesota when we were little, it was a fantasy come true.

How brilliant of my parents to come up with the idea of a cross country train ride! . We were all together, traveling west by train just as the first pioneers had done! Dad did not get tired from driving the car all day. Mom had packed sandwiches and treats for all of us in order to save money. Mike and Scott played games together in the diner car and I read most of the time. Denny enjoyed the scenery as he contemplated what his future would be like in a few short months.

For months, our parents must have saved the money they received from the laying hens' eggs and the milk from our cows in order to be able to give us this wonderful experience. We did not appreciate it adequately at the time but today, each of us savors the precious memories of this time together.

When Denny graduated from Navy boot camp, my parents went to San Diego to attend his graduation ceremony. He had been away for three months and it was the first time in my life that our family was minus one of us.

Denny was assigned to an Aircraft Carrier, the Coral Sea, for most of his four years of active duty. When my skinny, innocent, sweet and loving big brother returned home, he was no longer a kid. He was a grown man, and to some degree, a stranger. Denny's life was changed forever, as is probably true of most young people who come back from war.

In May of 1968, my brother, Denny, was stationed somewhere off the coast of Viet Nam. I had graduated from high school and was about to leave home and get started on the next chapter of my life.

Scott was upset that I was leaving home, so I asked him to care for my pet goldfish. I am not sure how long it was after I left that the goldfish died but, one day, Mom was doing her usual weekly cleaning when she noticed a terrible odor in Dad's office. She could not find the source yet continued to look throughout the day. Finally, my mom found a small white box in Dad's desk. Inside the box, wrapped in a soft, white tissue, was my very dead goldfish! Apparently, it had been there for several days.

Scott was asked why he had saved the little fish and placed it in the drawer. He told them that he was praying for it "to rise again." Every day he waited. Scott felt sure that it was just a matter of time before the fish would come back to life.

Such is the faith of a young child.

There were so many ways that Scott endeared himself to us. Before he could walk, Scott would ride around the house on this little white wooden horse with small red wheels. It had been handed down through the years from one cousin to the next, Mike first and then Scott, who was now the youngest. That little horse would squeak so loudly that we nicknamed the rider "Squeak," a name that stuck with Mike and Scott for quite a few years. Mother was quite happy to have her children riding around on that squeaky old toy, because she could easily identify where they were in the house. One out of four kids accounted for. All she had to do was listen for the squeaky little horse with the tiny, little boy on top, smiling his way on to the next adventure that was playing out in his head.

Scott and his first pup, Sandy--1963

Get Your Game On

Scott's growth spurt started when he was about eight or nine years old. About that time, our parents decided to move from the farm into town. Though Dad kept farming,

they bought a new house across the street from the ball diamond and golf course in our small town. Denny and I had already graduated from high school and were no longer living at home.

"The City Boys," Mike, Scott with Dad

With our family's move from the farm, Denny and I affectionately renamed Mike and Scott, "the city boys." They both began their careers in organized sports: T-ball, junior high basketball, baseball, football, and golf.

One of the great things about going to a small school was that everyone could try out for any activity they wanted. If you signed up for an extracurricular activity, chances were that you would get to play on a team and even excel at that activity. It was not uncommon for the stars on the basketball or football team to also be first chair in concert or marching band, be on the debate team or take a first at the State Speech Contest and, even sing in mixed chorus.

It was a wonderful feeling to be part of many different groups. This gave the young people in our town so much confidence. By the time of graduation, we were not afraid to step out of our comfort zones and stretch our proverbial wings as far as they would reach, and beyond.

Let the Music Play

Music was a large part of our family entertainment. Dad was an exceptionally good singer and dubbed, "Little Bing," when he was in his twenties. He even had a record cut while he was in the Navy and had it sent home to his parents as a Christmas gift. It was a recording of "I'll Be Home for Christmas." If you didn't know better, you would swear it was Bing himself singing to my grandparents!

Mom and Dad would teach us songs from the radio and, frequently, when we were driving to and from town, church, or relatives' houses, they would start a song. All four kids would join in, singing our four-part harmonies. We loved it and thought that, surely, one day we too would have our own TV show. Our family even had a radio that played in the barn when we milked our cows. Our dad was convinced that the volume of milk increased when the cows listened to soft music. The truth is, this idea worked. I think the cows felt the good vibrations via the radio. In turn, they were more relaxed, which naturally increased their milk

Jo Hamilton

production. How smart our dad was—way ahead of his time!

We found out at about three years of age, Scott could "carry a tune" and he loved to sing AND dance. Maybe because his dad had been in the Navy or maybe he just loved the song, but when the pop single "Blue Navy" hit the airwaves, Scott was all over it. He memorized the words immediately and would sing and dance to that song all day long. Heaven help anyone who stopped by for a visit. Before you could finish-saying "Hello," Scott would be asking you if you wanted to hear his new song. Once he started, it was hard to get him to stop. He knew all the verses and you would have to listen to ALL of them! His rhythm wasn't bad, either. He would rock from side to side, swaying with the beat as he sang the words. It was so cute and he was so serious about it, it still makes me smile just remembering that experience with him.

When Scott reached his teen years, he had become a promising athlete and a stellar student. He had also developed a love for fast cars and motorcycles. His adrenaline habit was ten times worse than any of the rest of us, or maybe all those "minor injuries" we had incurred throughout the years had dulled our addictive habits! When he was old enough to kick start a dirt bike, he taught himself to "pop a wheelie." He had been perfecting this technique over time on a smaller bike and gradually graduated to a 250 and then 500 cc motocross bike.

We have a picture of Scott riding his motorcycle on my brother Denny's wedding day. As he rides past my parents' house, we notice that the front wheel is off the ground. What most of my family did not see was that he had been riding on

Scott poppin' a wheelie on his bike

the rear wheel the entire length of that road, which was about a half mile! His technique was perfect. He was smiling the entire way in perfect balance. I am sure it was a thrill for him, but equally thrilling for me to observe.

Soon after that, Scott discovered rock and roll and became obsessed with learning to play the guitar. This also seemed to be a good way for him to meet and impress girls, which had become of great interest to him.

Whatever his motivation, Scott practiced and played guitar and, soon, he and a group of friends organized a local group called, "The Fulton Street Band". Scott was the lead guitarist and backup vocalist. He was now officially cool.

You Can Go Home

As Scott grew up, the miles between us widened. I became a medical technologist, moved to the East coast and went to work for the FBI. I was ready for some adventure and a break from farm life. Even though we did not see each other often, Scott and I remained close.

A few years later, while Scott was still in high school, I moved back to Iowa to start a business. I lived in the farmhouse where we grew up and on the land that my dad still farmed. For three years, I had the joy of watching Scott play high school football and baseball. He also became an all-state golfer, was vice president of his senior class and an honors student. Scott was named a High School Baseball All-American in 1979. I will forever be

Scott and his ride

grateful for those last few years that we had. It gave me additional time and memories with him I otherwise would have missed.

We had so much fun together, Scott and I. We labeled ourselves irreverently as the black sheep of the family. We loved to drive our cars and motorcycles fast, drag race at the quarter mile east of town and lay a patch of rubber on Main Street when backing out of a parking place. The local cop who was only on duty at night and weekends quickly put us on his watch list!

There were many, many memories that my family shared with our little brother. Scott had such high entertainment value and I try to keep that part of him alive by telling stories to my nieces and nephews who never had the chance to get to know him. Scott was joyful and mischievous, having a very understated but, large, personality.

After high school graduation, Scott attended Northwest Missouri State University on a baseball scholarship and pitched for the Bearcats. In 1981, he was invited to try out for the position of pitcher at the White Sox spring training camp. He earned a pitching position and

Scott, Northwest Bearcat

was invited back after his college graduation to take his shot in the minor leagues. He was having a great year! Scott's life was right on track. He loved baseball and, even though his plan was to get a degree in Industrial Engineering, his dream was to make his living playing baseball. He wanted to buy all of his siblings and his parents a new house one day!

It was about this time that Scott fell in love with the girl to whom he would remain forever connected. Though still in high school when they met, she would soon be propelled through life at warp speed, experiencing enough emotional pain and sorrow to last a hundred lifetimes.

Mom, Please Make Me an Appointment

It was the end of summer, August 1983, final call for
family vacations and carefree living. I had just purchased
my first home in Virginia and my parents and Scott were
coming to visit and check it out.

By now, Denny was out of the Navy and married with
two children. Following in our parents' footsteps, he was
trying his hand at farming, not far from our home place in
Iowa.

Mike had graduated from college and was newly
married. He and his wife were both working in Ames,
Iowa.

Scott and I had talked at length about what he would do
after he finished his last year of college should the baseball
plan fall through. We discussed the possibility of him and
his girlfriend moving to the East coast and living with me,
while they looked for jobs. I was excited about the
possibility of having family so close. The fact that it was
my baby brother was an added bonus!

For The Love of Scott!

I did not know that, before their planned trip East, Scott had been complaining about stomach and back pain to our mom. It was the summer between his junior and senior years of college. He was working on a construction site and playing baseball on two different teams in the evenings so no one thought too much about his having a few aches and pains. Mom called the doctor who had been treating our family for most of our lives and made Scott an appointment.

He went in, was examined, had an adjustment on his back and that was that. Scott never said anything to Mom about the visit, before or after.

A few days later, on a Wednesday evening, Mom called. I had been home for about two hours after finishing up my last teaching class of the day, and was grading papers when the phone rang. Mom was saying that Doc had called and told her that he had concerns about Scott. He had noticed a large lump in the area of Scott's groin. The doctor said that he did not know how Scott was able to walk around, let alone work full time and play ball two nights a week. Doc wanted him to see a specialist immediately.

Jo Hamilton

That was the beginning of what would soon become the worst nightmare of our lives. I received a phone call from Mom the day they were to leave on their trip East, telling me that Scott had to have exploratory surgery and that they would not be able to make the trip right now. In a few days, if everything went okay, they would be on their way.

The Fight Begins

August 11, 1983 was the day that Doc delivered the news. It was the day our summer came to a screeching halt and the long, tragic autumn began. This strong, handsome, athletic young man with his entire life ahead of him was in for the fight of his life.

Doc referred Scott to a surgeon in a much larger town an hour north of our family home. It had a bigger hospital with more specialized medical care available. Within a week, Scott had surgery to remove a testicular tumor along with his right testicle. There was also a mass in his abdomen that was inoperable. The tissue was biopsied and the results showed that Scott had testicular cancer, known as a nonseminomatous germ cell tumor.

For The Love of Scott!

The day of Scott's surgery came and went. I finally got the call about 9 pm EST. It was my Mom's voice on the other end of the phone. She sounded very calm, as she always did when she had to deliver bad news. This time however, something was different. She couldn't stop her heart from getting stuck in her words. Even though there was acceptance in her voice, there was something else unfamiliar to me. It was fear. She was scared of something and when she finally said the word, I knew why. It's the single word that changes entire lives in one swift second- Cancer, the big C, the killer, the fate sealer. To feel the instant helplessness under its powerful strength is overwhelming. I felt the anger of this disease with no distinction or prejudice. Anyone is fair game and it had just seized another victim. My little brother had cancer and he could die! He was so handsome, so strong and healthy looking. I knew it must be a mistake!

The doctors reassured us, Scott's prognosis was excellent, assuming that he would complete the recommended protocol of chemotherapy treatments. According to the medical experts, this type of cancer had a 90 + % cure rate, and Scott's cancer was discovered in an early stage. If he was destined to have cancer, at least it was a cancer with a high success factor. The fact that Scott was young, strong, and at the peak of physical health gave us more hope. His doctors and our family were optimistic that Scott would have a full recovery.

We were all committed to helping him through this challenge and come out on the other side as so many others have done—stronger, wiser, and better human beings for having survived the experience. We knew what had to be done. There was a plan, no crying, and no whining. Just do it! Together we could get through anything, just like when we were young.

Two days after his surgery, Scott called me. It would be the first of many long distance conversations that we would have during his treatment. Scott was optimistic but scared. I tried to reassure him that he would get the best of care, treatment, and medical expertise available in order for him to be healthy again. The surgeons in the Midwest hospital within an hour of our home were advising Scott to start chemo as soon as possible due to the aggressiveness of his type of cancer cells. He was leaning towards coming east and having it administered at Johns Hopkins or the National Institute of Health (NIH).

Scott's doctors, however, were all opposed to that plan, as were my parents. Everyone wanted him close to home in case he did not tolerate the chemotherapy drugs well. In the end, Scott gave in and decided to go to one of the most reputable hospitals in the Midwest. This hospital was still a four or five hour drive from home, but was world-renowned and considered the best place for treating Scott's cancer. So the decision was made and we all felt that Scott was on his way to a full recovery and a long, rich life.

By then, it was the middle of August. I decided to fly home and check on my baby brother. I needed to see him, ease his fear, wrap my arms around him, and try to keep him safe. He had some major decisions to make and he wanted to talk to me. Scott was one of the strongest forces of support and joy that I had in my life and I had never entertained a thought that he would become sick let alone suffer the effects of cancer.

At that time, I had been working in the medical field for a little over ten years. Based upon my hospital experience, I had become very pessimistic about the survival rates of those stricken with cancer. I had seen more cancer patients die than I could count, yet those patients were all convinced that they would be cured. Despite my fears, I had to see Scott to reassure him, and give him hope. I knew he would be different—we were ALL different now. .

The week was short and very tense. Everyone tried to act normal and happy, but our insides were churning with gut wrenching fear. Fear of the unknown, fear for Scott's life and what lie ahead for him. He looked so good. His 6'3" frame had finally filled out in all the right places. He actually had muscles. His eyes were bluer than I had remembered and his hair was more blond than usual from long days in the summer sun.

I remember thinking, God, he could be a model! There was that ever present smile, on that handsome rugged face, topped off by the deep dimple in his chin! I loved that face! I had studied every little detail over the years as I watched him grow and change. Even when he broke his nose during a high school basketball game, and chipped a tooth playing ice hockey, his face remained unchanged and as handsome as ever! Scott and I played a round of golf that provided an opportunity for some limited discussion about what he was thinking and feeling. This gave me a brief and understated glimpse into what Scott was going through. He wanted no sympathy or pity.

At one point, I noticed that Scott was smoking a cigarette, something I had never seen him do before. When I questioned him about it, he jokingly responded, "What are you afraid of? That it will give me cancer. Too late!"

Scott made it very clear to me that he did not want any of his

Saying good byes to Scott as he heads to 1st treatment, Aug 1983

friends to know about his diagnosis. He was so afraid that they would treat him differently and Scott did not want anyone worrying about or feeling sorry for him. It was bad enough that he was sick. Scott felt humiliated that his diagnosis was connected to his manliness and, even worse, that it was happening just as he was about to become engaged.

I tried to reason with him and reassure him that the support of his friends was as important as the support his family could give him and, that it was equally important for his friends. Scott would not budge from his stand. Who was I to argue with him? He was determined that he was going to get through this without a hitch and was sure that, by Christmas, we would all be celebrating the finale of this experience with all the joy, peace, and love which the season provided. The week passed quickly as our family tried to cherish each moment. Everything became more meaningful and urgent. Scott and I made plans to see each other again at Christmas. The testicular tumor was encapsulated. Even better, the surrounding lymph nodes and the other testicle were negative for any cancer cells. Scott's prognosis was very good at this point but with some uncertainty regarding the mass in his abdomen.

Our family was confused about what we had been told by the doctors. Was the mass a metastasis or a separate tumor? Was it related to his testicular cancer? I had to admit, I did not remember hearing of or knowing anyone dying from testicular cancer. I became more optimistic that everything was in place for Scott to win this fight and have a wonderful life.

As I headed back East, Scott and my parents were heading north for Scott's first meeting with his oncologist and his team of nurses. My spirit and heart traveled with them.

Let's Get This Party Started

Once at the hospital, Scott, his girlfriend and my parents received briefings regarding the chemotherapy treatments in order to help Scott make an informed decision.

Last family photo, Denny-Mike-Jo-Scott-Mom-Dad

The hospital oncology team counseled them on what to expect during and after each session: compromised immune system resulting in disease susceptibility, hair loss, sterility, nausea, and weight loss. They also asked Scott to volunteer for a clinical trial that would require submitting to more tests and blood draws than usual. The clinical trial would help the medical facility gather pertinent information on a relatively new chemo drug they would be using on Scott, called cisplatin. This appealed to Scott as his experience could potentially help others.

Scott was introduced to the nurses in the ward that would administer the new medication. These would be the nurses that he would have throughout the four treatment sessions. We were told that such consistency in staff made it easier for patients to develop a trusting relationship with the nurses. The staff would become familiar with patients' medications and dosages, thus reducing the risk of medication errors. They were the people who would provide the comfort and nurturing that was a critical part of each patient's healing and recovery. These nurses would come to know Scott better than anyone. They were his lifeline to restored health.

Scotts' sessions were scheduled to start the first week of the month and last for five full days. He would then have three weeks off to recover and rest and to get ready for the next session.

It seemed like a simple regimen, easy enough to follow. There would be only four chemotherapy sessions and, then, Scott would be home free. He would have, according to the experts, the guarantee of a 98 % cure rate at the end of those four sessions.

Scott had to make the decision whether or not to pursue this course of treatment. He had a lot to think about. The

oncology team gave him time to decide what, if anything, he wanted to do. Scott and his girlfriend walked around the lake at the hospital, feeding the

Scott feeding ducks by pond-Aug 83

ducks and geese. He spoke with some small children at the hospital who were receiving chemotherapy to treat their cancers.

Scott prayed and, by the end of the weekend, he had made his decision. How could he not do what everyone expected him to do?

On Monday, Scott started his first chemotherapy session. He took a deep breath, rolled up his sleeve and the treatments began. Scott lay there quietly watching as highly toxic drugs dripped into his arm. He was given a total of 55 mg of cisplatin and other medications over a 24-hour period. A nurse hung a new bag of cisplatin every eight hours and the liquid dripped continuously for five days. Each bag would contain 18.3 mg of cisplatin; the drug that would ultimately make his body well again, would first make him very, very ill.

Only Three More Months to Go

Scott tolerated the first couple of chemotherapy sessions better than most people. This was in part due to his 6'-3" and 190 lb. size, his age and his excellent physical condition. But, as predicted, the chemo sessions eventually took their toll. Scott lost his appetite just as his mouth developed raw, open sores and, as a result, his weight dropped. A few weeks after his first session, Scott started losing his hair so he asked Dad to shave his head and, then, they bought him a wig.

Winter was coming and Scott needed some protection for his head. I was at one of my favorite Virginia restaurants during this time, *Joe Theisman's*. Joe was the starting quarterback for the Washington Redskins in 1983.

He came into the restaurant that night, stopping by tables to chat with patrons. When he stopped by our table, I asked Joe if he could spare a hat for my little brother who was going through a rough time. He not only gave me a baseball cap but he also wrote a note on a 8"x10" photo for me to give to Scott, telling him to be strong, hang in there, and he would get through this battle.

As soon as he received that cap, Scott placed it on his head. We hardly ever saw him without the cap after that. In one of the last photos we took of Scott, he was wearing his Redskins baseball cap from quarterback Joe. I could never thank Joe Theisman enough for the joy and the big smile that single act of kindness gave to my brother!

I called Scott after his first chemo session was completed and he shared with me some of the horrendous after effects. His nausea continued for nearly a week after the treatment stopped, leaving him very weak. Still, Scott had no doubt that the treatment was all going to be worth it. What choice did he have?

My parents had purchased a used Chevy custom van to transport Scott more comfortably to and from his treatments. Every three weeks, Scott and my parents drove

Jo Hamilton

five hours in their van to the hospital, the Mecca of Medicine. Scott was given his cycle of drugs, which, in theory, would wipe out all the cancer cells. In the process, those drugs would also compromise his immune system due to the depletion of his good, white fighter cells. Despite the pain and suffering, this treatment was Scott's chance to regain his life.

Scott's second treatment began in September, the week of his 23rd birthday. I sent him a Walkman® and some cassettes so that he could fill his head with the sweet sounds of Stevie Nicks, Santana, Journey, and other music he loved, while the poison dripped into his bloodstream. I wanted to help Scott get through those long five days of chemotherapy any way I could. He needed something pleasant to focus upon while he watched the drip, drip, drip of the cisplatin flowing into his body. During the process, Scott would count down the hours until he would again no longer be tethered to the IV bottle that kept him hostage for those painfully long five days.

Scott's veins were already starting to corrode from the toxicity of the chemotherapy. The sclerosis in his veins was becoming visible even to a layperson. He made many friends in the Oncology Ward, known among the patients as, "the ward of the living dead." There were many people, young and old alike, on the same treatment schedule as Scott. These patients had an unspoken bond that none of us on the outside would ever truly understand. So many of the people who Scott met were terminally ill and knew they would not make it to another year. Scott became especially close to the younger children with cancer. He would spend time reading books to the children, walking with them by the pond to feed the geese and ducks and telling them jokes. Scott would try to make them laugh and forget their pain and illness. In return, the children taught him some of his most valuable life lessons. They were open and nonjudgmental, totally living in the moment. The children did not worry about their illnesses because they knew nothing about death or dying and, thus, they gave Scott faith and hope.

In between each five-day session, Scott would go back to work at his construction job even though he was weak and exhausted. He needed to maintain some kind of normalcy and control when so much in his life was out of his control.

Jo Hamilton

One day, my Mom received a call from Scott's job supervisor telling her that Scott had passed out at work and was not doing well. Someone needed to come and drive him home. The next day, Scott was back at work apologizing for having to take time off from the previous day. He wanted to pull his own weight and not be perceived by anyone as being weak.

After his third chemo session, another CAT scan was performed which showed that the abdominal tumor was gone! The drugs had done their job. His blood cell markers were normal. Scott was in complete remission. He was cancer free! Everyone was ecstatic, especially Scott.

The news came right before the Thanksgiving holiday and we all felt as though the weight of the world had been lifted from our shoulders. Scott had made it through the terrible chemo treatments alive. His body had fought off the dreaded cancer. Scott would have his life back!

Everyone had a hearty appetite that holiday. Even Scott had two helpings of mash potatoes and gravy.

The doctors told Scott that he was in complete remission. His cancer cell markers were at zero.

Only one more treatment to go!

The Beginning of the Ninth

The doctors had another meeting with my parents, Scott, and his girlfriend, indicating they were very pleased with the results that were being seen. Scott's cancer cell markers were perfect. The CAT scan was totally negative! His abdomen was tumor-free. As far as Scott was concerned, he slid into home plate and was safe. Last inning, game over! Goodbye to cancer!

I was in Virginia on that Thanksgiving Day and would be joining everyone for the Christmas holiday and, the end-of-chemo celebration that we had planned for Scott.

Last Thanksgiving-Scott (l) wearing Redskins ball cap-Nov 1983

After everyone had finished their meal back in Iowa, I received a phone call from Mom and Dad. All my brothers and their families were calling to say hello and to wish me a Happy Thanksgiving.

I spoke with Scott last. He was upset. The doctors wanted him to go ahead and complete the fourth and final round of chemo as sort of an insurance policy. They had told Scott that he would never have to worry about getting cancer ever again in this lifetime—it was a 99.9 % certainty! Still, Scott was angry. He felt deceived. He had fulfilled his initial contract and now he was in complete remission! Why should he listen to them and have to endure another month of torture?

This did not make any sense to Scott and he really did not want to do it. His voice started to quiver as he said, "Why should I go through five more days of hell if the cancer is already gone?"

I felt sad, angry, and helpless. How dare they promise him life and then make another condition for him to have to follow, pulling the gold ring a little further away? It seemed cruel and confusing to me. My parents had also questioned if Scott really needed the final treatment since the doctors had told us that he was in complete remission.

Mom and Dad asked the doctors if Scott could receive his treatment at a hospital in a different city much closer to home. The hospital staff rather arrogantly cautioned my parents against this idea. It would be much better, they had insisted, to administer and monitor the drugs that were, as they had described them, "Like a loaded shotgun," at their more sophisticated center

My family and I spent the better part of an hour trying to sort it all out. Close to the end of our phone call, Scott asked me what I would do. I hesitated to say anything but, finally, I said, "It is only five more days, Scott. Compared to the rest of your life and not having to live in constant fear and worry about the cancer coming back, it might be worth it." If the experts were saying that Scott would be cured with an almost 100 % guarantee, how could our family argue with that?

In the end, I told Scott that this was his life and that he had to do what was best for him. None of us could make that choice for him.

Scott was still not sure if he would go through with the final chemo treatment. He really wanted someone to tell him what to do but, in his heart, he felt that the doctors were giving him no choice. He was not going to have anyone say or think that he had not given his all. Scott was never a quitter and he did not intend to lose *this* game. The stakes were too high and he was still young.

If I could have the same conversation with Scott today, I would wholeheartedly agree with his initial choice and tell him to pass on the doctors' final suggestion. I would tell Scott that his gut feeling was right on target. Dead right!

The Beginning of the End

Despite a fierce Iowa blizzard, my parents and Scott headed back to the hospital so that Scott could start his final round of chemotherapy. Scott was eager to get it behind him. He was sick and tired of being sick and tired.

Before his last cycle began, Scott asked his team of doctors about the possibility of receiving all his chemo in one day. He rationalized that he would rather feel horrible for a day or two than drag the torture out through the entire week. They explained that this would be physically impossible. Cisplatin was too toxic and lethal to be administered that quickly into his system. The result would be a catastrophic and a life-ending overdose.

This drug was so toxic that it was monitored by the NIH. Nurses that were of childbearing age were not allowed to go near this drug or had to sign a waiver. Scott had several small burn scabs on his hands, arms and chest that had occurred when the needle dripped this caustic liquid onto those areas when being taken out of his veins after his chemo cycle was completed.

Scott's veins resembled old pipes clogged by years of hard water. They were corroded and hard to the touch. These were just some of the side effects of cisplatin.

Many times in my years as a medical technologist, I had heard doctors say, "If they can survive the treatment, they will have a fighting chance."

The sad truth was that many people who were already weakened from surgery and with compromised conditions did not have the physical strength to endure the grueling effects of chemotherapy. Scott had made it through those first three sessions for many reasons. He was young and physically fit, had great support from family, and had deep faith. Plus, Scott trusted his doctors and nurses. He was a fighter and he believed that suffering through the chemo sessions was all going to be worth it.

In the end, Scott finally persuaded the doctors to speed up the rate of medicine drip so that he could finish a half day earlier. On December 2, 1983, Scott's last session of chemo began. The first bag of cisplatin was hung just as it had been done many times before by the same team of nurses who had cared for him during his previous three treatments. The prescribed dosage of cisplatin had not changed in the last three months. Scott had been treated with 18.3 mg in each bag, three times a day. Each bag would drip for eight hours and then another hung for the same length of time.

Finally, the last bag of the day was started, making the amount of cisplatin that Scott received in a 24-hour period exactly 55 mg. The IV bag looked as harmless as sugar water when the nurses placed it on the IV stand. With the IV stand, Scott had the luxury of moving around if he felt well enough to do so.

Within the first 24 hours of the five day session, Scott started vomiting. This was unusual for him so soon into the treatment, but Scott's nurse felt that the vomiting was an emotional reaction or, perhaps, because they had sped up the drip flow. Soon, my parents noticed a change in the color of the pigment in Scott's hands. They alerted the nurse of a possible complication. Although this development had not presented itself before, the nurse casually passed off the change in color as Scott being excessively excited about finishing his chemo early. "Perhaps his body was just overreacting," they said.

On the second day, Scott felt much worse. My parents kept insisting that something was wrong. When the doctors made their rounds, Scott repeatedly asked them to stop the treatment. He even pleaded with my parents to have them abort the chemo session.

At one point, my father yelled, "Take the damn needle out or I'll do it myself!" The nurses and doctors all left Scott's room. They needed to consult with one another about what to do.

The medical professionals acknowledged Scott's anxiety and anguish, recorded it on his chart, prescribed Valium and insisted that the treatment must continue. The doctors reminded my parents that Scott had signed up for a trail study and that it was critical for him to continue so that the data gathered could benefit others with the same cancer.

Poor Mom and Dad did not know it then, but they had become both unwitting accomplices and tragic victims.

When Scott complained that he could not feel his body, Dad told him that the doctors had given him their total assurance that the treatment was necessary for the study and total eradication of the cancer. Scott felt that he could not fight the doctors and the chemo, so he finally succumbed to their wishes.

Not one of the doctors or nurses bothered to investigate further or check to see if it might be the drugs that were contributing to these bizarre symptoms.

We know now that Scott and my parents' requests to repeatedly stop his treatment and thus, end the trial in which he was participating, was completely and blatantly disregarded by his doctors. My family had no idea that Scott was protected by the Common Rule and the FDA regulations that provide protection for human subjects in research studies. The first time that Scott and my father asked the doctors to stop the treatment, it should have immediately ceased. The doctors knew that every time they argued and eventually convinced my parents and Scott to continue treatment, they were violating Federal Law. Yet, they continued to pressure him and my parents. This is another huge lesson for all of us to remember when trying to keep ourselves and those we love, safe from medical harm. No means NO!

On the third day of his final session, Scott fearfully announced that he could not hear. When he tried to head to the bathroom, Scott realized that he could not stand up. Each time, he would fall and Dad would have to assist him. Eventually Scott became

> He screamed, "I feel like I'm dying. I can't feel my body anymore!"

so weak that he would not even attempt to make it into the bathroom, resorting to the use of a urinal at his bed. It was then that our father noticed that Scott's urine had a very strong metallic and unpleasant odor.

Again, my parents asked the nurse about these symptoms, but those questions were quickly dismissed.

Scott kept complaining to the nurses about all the things that were different from his previous sessions. Instead of investigating, the nurses simply kept on administering pain-killing drugs. Scott kept questioning the nurses about the

Jo Hamilton

wisdom of injecting more medications into his body. He tried to refuse the drugs but none of the medical staff would listen.

On the fourth day, Scott begged the nurses to stop the chemo. He screamed, "I feel like I'm dying. I can't feel my body anymore!"

His ears were constantly ringing and he had no strength. Scott's girlfriend had to leave the room because she was so emotionally distraught.

The team of expert doctors came in and talked Scott into continuing the treatment for just one more day. He felt so helpless against them. Scott worried that if he did not do what the doctors asked, the cancer would return and his life would be shortened. His vitals were stable for the time being so, under extreme pressure from the medical team; Scott agreed to continue the chemo for 24 more hours.

Sadly, the worst was still ahead of him.

The last day of chemo treatment was extremely long and full of excruciating pain but, finally, Scott finished the last bag of Cisplatin. As the nurse unhooked him from the IV, she congratulated Scott and exclaimed, "Way to go Scott. You did it!"

For The Love of Scott!

This day was the first time after all his treatments that
Scott had to be pushed out of the hospital in a wheel chair.
My parents, Scott and his girlfriend drove back to their
hotel where they planned to spend the night and then leave
early the next morning for home. Normally they would
return home right after Scott was discharged. This time
because he was so ill, they decided to wait until morning to
see if his condition improved. Scott was thrilled and
relieved to be finished and, he was also very emotional. He
could now pursue his dreams in good health and happiness,
or so we thought.

My dad was so proud of Scott. He looked forward to
Scott's full recovery and the possibility of a pro baseball
career for his beloved, youngest son.

The truth is that my dad and Scott had not always been
close. Scott had been a challenging teenager. He would
push the envelope every chance he got. Being the youngest
was hard but Scott was also the most gifted and easily
became bored. He made some choices that my parents did
not always approve. When Scott became ill, the
relationship shifted between him and Dad. Scott grew up
and Dad opened up. Going through chemo with Scott gave

Jo Hamilton

our father a completely new respect for Scott and expanded his heart in ways that he could never have imagined.

During his diagnosis and hospitalization, Scott had managed to persuade Dad to give up his smoking habit, a habit of his since his stint in the Navy. Scott and Dad had both accomplished so much through this challenging time and now we could all celebrate.

Once they were all back to the hotel and settled in for the night, Scott became very thirsty. He drank glass after glass of water and then started craving milk. He kept complaining that his throat felt like it was on fire. Shortly after that announcement, Scott said that he felt hungry and would like to eat something. My parents were excited to think that; maybe, Scott was getting his appetite back. Then, Scott started vomiting all the water and milk that he had drunk.

Dad suggested that maybe a bath would help relax him and settle him down. It was also a way to get him cleaned up. So, into the tub Scott went.

Scott became increasingly ill with violent bouts of projectile vomiting and, soon, he was too weak to get out of the tub. Scott was 6'-3." Our mother was 5'-5" and 120 pounds and my dad was 5'-10" and 160 pounds. Even with the help of Scott's girlfriend, it was all they could do to get him back to the bed.

Everyone became increasingly concerned. Scott was confused and frightened. This was uncharted territory for all of them. Mom called the hospital but no one there seemed very concerned. The staff said that Scott was probably suffering from dehydration or emotional aftershock and then told Mom and Dad not to worry. My parents were told to only call back if the vomiting continued. They kept vigil throughout the night, watching Scott's condition deteriorate.

Finally, in the early morning hours, everyone in the room knew that this was not some psychosomatic response to a final chemo treatment. All they had to do was look at Scott. He was gray in color and too weak to sit up or raise his head. Scott was growing increasingly confused about his condition, yet he still had faith that the doctors could fix whatever was wrong. Mom placed a second call to the hospital. This time she asked for an ambulance to be sent to the hotel. My parents were told there was no ambulance available to bring Scott back to the hospital. Mom insisted they do something or they were going to lose him! A few minutes later, a white panel work van showed up at the hotel. It had no windows, no carpet, and no heat. It was 40 below zero!

My parents and Scott's girlfriend somehow managed to get him downstairs and loaded into the back of the van. He had no blankets or pad to lie on, but they had a ride back to the hospital. Dad helped him into a folding chair they found in the back and somehow managed to keep him upright and steady, until they arrived at the emergency room entrance. Where did the van come from? The hospital hadn't sent it.

No questions were asked by the medical personnel. They hadn't expected to see Scott back again.

You're Out!

Scott was immediately taken to the Intensive Care Unit.

My family was told that the ICU was necessary because it had the required equipment to monitor his condition.

["I *know* it's the chemo!"] Scott was begging the staff to, "Please, get me there quickly." When he finally got to look into the familiar face of one of his doctors, Scott said, "It's the chemo, isn't it? I know it's the chemo! I feel like I'm dying. I can't feel my body any more. I *know* it's the chemo!"

Scott's doctor grabbed his hand and said, "We do not know what is wrong yet, Scott, but trust me, you are not going to die. We will get this figured out."

Scott's chart was pulled, notes were reviewed, and medications were recalculated. The pharmacology sheet was sent to the pharmacy with the hope that they might find an answer.

Still in Virginia on December 8th, I placed a call to my parents' house in Iowa. I knew that Scott was to have been dismissed from his final chemo session on December 7th and I was eager to see how he was doing. I wanted to congratulate Scott for being so brave and strong, and for making it through his toughest chemo session yet. Also, December 9th was my mother's birthday and I wanted to give her an early birthday wish. I anticipated that she was already celebrating!

There was no answer the first, second or third time that I called, which seemed very odd to me. I called my middle brother, Mike, to see if he knew where everybody was. He informed me that he had briefly spoken with Mom and was told that Scott had some complications during the last treatment. I learned that after being dismissed on December 7th, Scott had to be readmitted to the ICU on the following day.

Mike also told me that Scott was having trouble with his hearing and could not keep anything in his stomach. I learned that Scott had become so dehydrated that he went into shock and started hemorrhaging in his stomach. Mike gave me the phone number for Scott's room. When I called, a woman that I did not know answered the phone. After explaining to her that I was Scott's sister from Virginia, I asked to speak with him. The woman informed me that she was his nurse and that he was unable to come to the phone.

I asked her, "Why? Was there a problem?"

It was then that she suggested that I speak with my parents. Questions bombarded my brain. Where were they? Why were they not with Scott? What was going on? Why couldn't he come to the phone?

I called my oldest brother, Denny, who had just come through an operation of his own. He was able to give me another phone number for my parents. They were staying in a hotel close to the hospital. Denny, always the cool, calm, serene force in the family, reassured me that everything was going to be okay and Scott was a lot better now.

Alarms were going off in my head. I knew in my gut that something was dreadfully wrong. Immediately I made reservations to fly home to Iowa early the next morning. It was close to our Christmas break at the school where I was teaching so I called and received permission to leave early due to a family emergency.

I then called my parents. Mom sounded tired, worried, and sad. She told me that Scott could not hear and was extremely weak. I told my mom that I would be coming home early the next morning.

My brother, Mike, and his wife met me at the airport and we drove five hours to our final destination. All of us were filled with anxiety and apprehension as to what we would find. I had not seen Scott since August when he had been the picture of health and vitality. We drove through frigid temperatures and whiteouts accompanied by strong winds, pelting snow, and a wind-chill of minus 40 degrees, but we finally arrived safely at the medical facility. Because winters in that area are often harsh, there are underground tunnels that allow patients, medical personnel,

Jo Hamilton

and, visitors access to each building without having to endure the elements.

Once inside the hospital, we found that no one seemed to know where our little brother was. We searched for a long time before finally locating a nurse who told us that Scott had been moved to a room that would offer him better protection.

"From what?" we asked.

It seemed that Scott's white blood count was dangerously low. The normal values should be from 5,000 to 10,000 cells per centimeter (c/cm). Scott's level had dropped below 100 c/cm. The room into

{ His skin was orange, the color of a new basketball. }

which he had been placed was continuously circulating fresh air in and out in order to keep the air pure and bacteria free.

The nurse pointed us toward a hallway. Mike, his wife, and I headed down the corridor in the direction of Scott's room.

We heard screams. The closer we came to Scott's room, the louder the screams became. When we stopped in front of the large observation windows, we saw something that is forever etched in our memories. There lay our baby brother. His skin was orange, the color of a new basketball. Scott's once-handsome face was contorted by pain. It was magnified by the stark baldness of his beautiful, round head. There were tubes coming out of his wrists and the brachial arteries in his shoulders. He was on oxygen.

The most tragic and disturbing thing of all was to see Scott pounding on his chest with his fists, screaming to be put to sleep, to be given more medicine, and crying out, "Please, stop the pain!"

The three of us were frozen, unable to move another step, locked in a cruel trance as we watched blood shoot from Scott's mouth.

The doctor motioned us in. We had to put on gowns and masks before entering the room. Scott was speaking very loudly due to his hearing loss. Despite being in a painful and horrific state, in a very loud voice, Scott asked Mike how he was doing. Mike answered him, "I'm fine, how 'bout you?"

Scott replied, "I'm good." We could clearly see that was not the case.

Mike turned and ran out of Scott's room and down the hall in tears, his wife following close behind. I turned my attention back to Scott and what was going on in that room. Scott's eyes were so glazed over with pain that he looked like a wild man. He was writhing around on the bed, finding no relief anywhere. "What in the world was going on?" I thought. Something awful had happened to Scott and we did not know what it was.

As I left Scott's room looking for my parents, I saw them step off the elevator. They had been at mass in the Chapel, praying. When they looked up and saw us, Mom started to cry. About the same time, a nurse came down the hallway saying that, THEY wanted to have a meeting with the family.

The hospital administrator, head oncologist, and other staff met with our family in the nurses' lounge. They had already had a brief conversation with my parents earlier in the day. The oncologist told us that they had finally discovered what was causing Scott's unbearable condition. It had taken them three days after his readmission and, not until forced to investigate, to find the reason behind the symptoms that Scott had been exhibiting for eight days.

Scott had been given a cisplatin overdose.

The first question out of my mouth was, "How much of an overdose?"

We all knew that Scott was to have been given three bags of chemo a day, totaling 55 mg per day. This time, however, the pharmacist in charge of mixing Scott's medication had made an irreversible error. He had mixed

> He had received *15 times* more cisplatin than was ordered.

each of Scott's bags with an entire day's dose of 55 mg! Not one nurse or doctor who had hung the bags had ever checked the labels. If someone had, they would have clearly seen that the bags contained three times the amount they should have contained. Scott had been given three of those bags a day for five days. He had received *15 times* more cisplatin than was ordered. Instead of 275 mg total for five days, as he had received in each of his past three treatments, this time he had received a total dosage of 825 mg.

Unknown to the medical team at the time, the staff HAD administered Scott's last treatment very quickly. He had been given his entire five days of chemotherapy in 1 ½ days and then another 3 ½ additional days of chemo on top of that!

The head oncologist said, "We will accept full responsibility for the mistake and do everything that we can to save Scott. We are amazed that he is still alive."

"Medically speaking, he should not have lived past the first two days of treatment. He has already surprised us. Scott is a strong young man, a fighter."

The doctor continued, "He has the best people in the

> *"**For the love of Scott!** How could this have happened?"*

world working on him. We have called in experts from all over the world to help us but this has never happened before and we really do not know what we are dealing with here. It will be an hour-by-hour vigil."

We did not understand then that those hours would drag on into days, and the days into nights, and the nights into weeks.

The last thing I heard was, "We are so sorry."

Tears, cries of disbelief, and unbelievable pain followed for all of us after that meeting.

My mom, her heart broken in half, cried, *"**For the love of Scott!** How could this have happened?"*

I remember that I wanted to kick something, someone, anything but my legs felt too weak to move. Mike walked around clenching and unclenching his fists. He was very angry. It was at that moment we decided, from that day forward, to monitor my baby brother's environment as much as humanly possible. The word, trust, was no longer a part of our vocabulary in relation to these people. The medical staff had already made one grandiose, devastating mistake. How many more would there be?

Jo Hamilton

His House
12-16-83

Where can he live when his body collapses?
He has no other house!
They've poisoned his walls, his windows, his floors.
But his furnace still roars with the force of a fuel
so far from within,
they haven't yet found the way to extinguish the blaze.
They're sorry . . . everyone is sorry,
Scott doesn't know he is dying.
With faith you come here, for the very best of care,
and it's home you are sent in a box.
The smell of Death is so strong,
it oozes from all the cold and haunted places.
It fills up the living with so much pain,
you can't bear to look in their faces.
I could look for a thousand answers
to questions that don't really matter.
My Brother came here to get well,
and instead by mistake they have killed him!
Jo Hamilton

The Death Vigil

Watching someone you love die is like watching a movie in black and white. Even the sound is muted. Days and nights run together and time is measured by the change in the shifts of the nurses that come and go. Your senses become dull. You force yourself to eat but nothing has any taste. As you become sleep deprived, your brain stays in a perpetual fog.

Our family unit was broken. Each of us turned within ourselves to our own private thoughts, separated by emotional walls so thick that we could not acknowledge the reality that we were living. Hugs were hollow, words were empty, and movement was mechanical. Only Scott mattered. Our family worked out a schedule where I would stay with Scott at night and my parents, Mike and his wife, would come during the day to protect him from any more medical harm. I knew deep inside my heart that, without a miracle, he was already dead.

The doctors came into his room during the day with updates on Scott's condition. Somehow, they found out that I worked in the medical field so the doctors began to speak directly to me. Then, in a patronizing manner, they would give me a pat on the shoulder and say, "There now, you can explain all this to your folks," as though my parents were incompetent human beings who could not understand what was being said. This behavior was infuriating to me, painful and very disrespectful. I wondered if those doctors felt so much guilt over the way that they had emotionally beaten up and pressured our parents to ignore their instincts, that they could no longer bear to look Mom and Dad in the eye.

At night, there were many medical personnel stopping by Scott's room when it was quiet and less hectic. I had grown up enthralled with the medical field. For most of my young life, I had fully intended to become a doctor. I had helped birth and care for more animals than I could remember. Everything about the human body had always fascinated me.

Up to this point in my life, I had had nothing but wonderful experiences and loving memories of hospitals, doctors, and nurses. While working as a medical technologist in a small hospital, I had spent more holidays and nights with the nurses than I had with my own family.

For The Love of Scott!

It was so difficult for me to comprehend how this chemo mistake could have possibly happened to my brother, not just once or twice, but three times with three different nurses, every day for four and a half days.

Every nurse who had picked up the bag of Scott's chemo had looked at the bag, with it clearly labeled as 55 mg instead of 18.3 mg, wrote 18.3 mg on his chart, and hung it on the IV stand. "Or had they?" I often wondered. The nurses had watched the chemo drip into Scott's veins for eight hours, changed the bag and then, hung another, every shift. Each nurse had ignored the classic toxicity signs of a cisplatin drug overdose even when my parents and Scott had insisted that there was something horrifically wrong.

I felt awful for those nurses. I felt betrayed by them. I had such strong faith in the medical system and had witnessed first-hand the marvel of modern medicine and the miracles that it had regularly produced.

I could not yet wrap my mind around the emotions that I now felt about this profession, one that I had loved so much.

Jo Hamilton

On one of the first nights I stayed with Scott, he seemed more agitated than usual. Pulling my chair up close to Scott's bed, I wiped his forehead and then held his hand while trying desperately to sooth him. When my efforts did not help, I lay down beside Scott in his bed and softly sang to him just as I had done when he was a baby.

> "Jo, you have to tell people what they've done to me. *You have to tell them*!"

He was still in so much pain. Through his labored breath, he said, "Jo, you have to tell people what they've done to me. *You have to tell them*!"

Those were the last rational words Scott would say to me.

A few nights later, he was flailing around in pain, very distraught, still unable to get any relief. He kept telling me, "We need to take care of the house. Make sure she gets the house and keeps it."

This had no significant meaning to me until I shared it with my parents the next day. They recalled Scott telling them that, once he made the major leagues, he was going to buy everyone in the family a new house. Despite the level of pain that Scott was enduring, somewhere in his mind the thought of caring for his family was still predominate in his psyche.

There was always a steady stream of nurses coming and going every night. I cannot begin to tell you the level of despair and suffering they were experiencing. These nurses were the caretakers, the healers, who had been with Scott and my parents since the beginning of his chemo sessions. They had fought this cancer side-by-side with him and wiped his brow when he was feeling sick and vomiting from the chemotherapy. These nurses had shared with Scott their stories, jokes, life experiences, and tears. Some were close in age to him. The nurses were Scott's best cheerleaders when he was depressed and were here to take care of him, protect him, and help him to heal.

Yet, because of their errors, these nurses now had to bear witness to Scott's constant battle to live through another hour, another day and, at best, a lifetime tethered to numerous machines that would breathe for him, take nourishment in for him, and clean his blood for him. Even if he survived, Scott would never again throw a pitch, hit a home run, or slide his long, lanky legs safely into home plate. His dream of a future in the major leagues was rapidly fading from our minds as we watched his body fade farther from life day by day.

Right before Christmas, my cousins, Steve and Georgeann, drove Denny up to see Scott and to be with our family. They had to dodge another Midwest blizzard in order to arrive safely. Having had recent surgery himself, Denny was not yet allowed to drive.

Mom was adamant that we not tell other people how grave Scott's condition was so it was a horrible shock to them when they finally saw Scott. I think Mom's theory was that, if we did not talk aloud to anyone else about his condition, maybe it was not really happening. We could ignore how sick Scott really was and maybe, just maybe, he would recover.

My cousin, Steve, had been a medic during the Viet Nam war. He came out of Scott's room visibly shaken. His wife, Georgeann, decided that she could not go in. Steve had told her that, of all his years in Viet Nam, he had never experienced anything as horrendous as what Scott was going through. Steve would not go into Scott's room again.

By this time, the medical staff had Scott restrained and drugged with a paralyzing medication in order to prevent him from moving. This was done to ensure that he would not pull out the IV lines that were progressively getting harder and harder to place. Scott had started hemorrhaging from his nose, eyes, ears, and throat. Blood was leaking into his lungs and pericardium, the sac surrounding his heart. The nurses had placed little cups over Scott's eyelids in order to keep his eyes moist since he could no longer blink.

The doctors told us that if we spoke loud enough, Scott could still hear us. He certainly could feel our energy around him. Scott was still feeling pain but could no longer express it with his body. So, the medical staff created an illusion for us. Even though the cisplatin was slowly and deliberately eating its way through the inside of Scott's body, we no longer had to be uncomfortable when looking at him because he appeared calmer and more at peace.

Our family would soon learn that even wonder drugs can fool the human body for only so long. Scott's body was fighting with everything it had in order to fix what they had done to his human machine.

Homeostasis is the word used to describe what our body attempts to do in order to maintain balance when something happens to invade, attack, or disrupt it. Scott's body had not given up yet and neither had we.

The Last Christmas

Every day, I would come in and pick up Scott's chart from the end of the bed and review his test results. I started educating my family about the equipment that was surrounding Scott's world. I taught them what to look for when observing the machines in his room and what questions to ask the nurses when they were drawing his blood. Such questions were so important. What were they doing to Scott? What tests were they checking? What were the results?

The questions helped to make the doctors and nurses accountable for their actions and helped to ensure us they were paying attention. It also gave my family some much needed control and a sense that they were doing SOMETHING to keep Scott safe. We would no longer be "brushed off" by any of the medical personnel—we wanted answers to all of our questions, and the answers had better make sense or there would be more questions to follow!

I also went over with my family what to look for on Scott's chart. It was not long before all of us were discussing his WBC, HBG, HCT, BUN, and electrolyte levels. We kept track of when his next dialysis was scheduled and the status of his O^2 levels and percentages. We wanted to know, "How good are Scott's blood gas levels?"

Every time medical personnel would come into Scott's room, they were bombarded with questions from our family. We all needed a task in order to feel useful and to ease our frustration and guilt. Around December 17th or 18th, due to Scott's deteriorating respiratory condition, the doctors decided to place him on a ventilator. He would not be able to speak. We were told that once Scott's condition improved, he would be removed from the breathing device.

Scott's white blood cell count continued to decline and the fluid that was filling his lungs would later progress into pneumonia. The oxygen content was kept on 60 % or higher to ensure that his brain and organs were getting enough of the precious air that they so desperately needed. There were times when Scott continued to be quite agitated while on the ventilator. Another drug was administered to keep him sedated enough to not fight the breathing device.

As our family sat and watched Scott's occasional struggle against the restraints on his hands and feet, we often wondered, "Was there something that Scott was trying to say, some message that he needed to share?" This remains an unanswered question, as we never heard him speak another word.

We were all sitting together at the hospital on Christmas Eve, preoccupied with worry. All of us were mindlessly watching television until we began to listen to TV reports about the young figure skater named Scott Hamilton, a Gold Medal hopeful in the Winter Olympic Games.

Scott Hamilton? Really? We were hearing an amazing story about this young man. He had been adopted at six weeks of age by a couple in Ohio. At the age of two, this Scott had contracted a mysterious disease that caused him to stop growing. After numerous tests and several misdiagnoses, one being cystic fibrosis, the doctors had told his family he had only six months to live. Then, suddenly, the condition began to correct itself. The news commentators were reporting was that a special diet and exercise had contributed to an eventual cure. However, this Scott Hamilton grew to be only 5'-2 ½" inches in height and weighed only 108 lbs. during his peak skating years.

All of us felt instantly bonded to this young athlete, not just because of his name and the fact that he was only two years older than our Scott Hamilton was, but because he, too, had fought the odds. This Scott had come through his ordeal healthy, happy, full of life, and able to fulfill his dreams.

Even as we marveled at the story of Scott Hamilton, the Olympic skater, we knew that *our* Scott Hamilton would never see his dreams come true.

To add to my sadness, I had been visited the night before by one of Scott's favorite nurses. She had stopped at Scott's room just to talk. Ever since we had been told of the chemo overdose, there had been a trail of his nurses wanting to apologize, to ask forgiveness, or to just sit with him. This was a very uncomfortable situation at times and, as much as a part of me wanted to help them feel better, there was nothing I could say or do that was going to make any part of Scott's situation better. I had my own issues to deal with and was angry and upset with all of them.

I asked each one individually how this terrible error could possibly have happened. These nurses were highly skilled and trained professionals in the specialty field of oncology and were working in one of the most prestigious hospitals in the world. The most common answer each nurse gave to me was, "This is a hospital of checks, rechecks, and cross-checks. I assumed, since everyone is always checking everything, someone had already checked the bags, the labels, the dosage and that meant everything was fine."

Instead of reviewing the chart and chemo bag amounts for themselves, they had each believed that someone else had already done the checking. In other words, these nurses just assumed that everything was fine and proceeded as usual. If a mistake had been made, each one figured that someone else would have caught it.

Three nurses a day and half a dozen doctors over a five-day period had assumed that "someone else" had checked the medication, the dosage, and the label on the Cisplatin bag. Each one had signed Scott's chart, repeatedly, as a statement that everything was okay. In reality, not one of them had ever looked.

This time, the medical staffs' assumptions had resulted in an irreversible, fatal medical error. The hospital, with all of its brilliant doctors and nurses, checks and balances, and Hippocratic Oath to "Do no harm," had somehow managed to overlook the classic textbook signs of toxicity poisoning. For five full days, they had ignored the pleas from Scott and from my parents to, "Help him."

On Christmas Eve, I had gone back to the private room that had been reserved for our family where we could to go rest. There was a knock at the door. There stood another one of Scott's oncology team nurses, crying very hard. She kept asking me to please forgive her. She said, "If Scott dies, I am a murderer!"

At the time, I could not have agreed with her more, but I thought, "How can I say that to her?"

A few hours later during our Christmas Eve vigil, one of the attending doctors on call, came into the patients' lounge where we were gathered, listening to Christmas carols. He told us that it was time to call a priest in order to offer Scott the last rites. We all gathered in Scott's room standing around his bed. Mom and Dad were on either side of Scott's head and the rest of us were along his sides, touching and holding onto him

As the priest was making the sign of the cross, lighting candles, praying and burning incense, Scott opened his eyes and looked at each of us. Tears were running down the sides of his face. "How could this be?" we wondered. Scott was paralyzed and could not move any part of his body yet he was moving his eyes. His eyes seemed to be pleading to us all as though to say, "Don't give up on me yet. I'm not done fighting. I still want to live, you guys!"

Scott's heart stopped beating and then started again, stopped and started again and, this time, it continued to beat. The priest left and we all stayed there with him through the rest of the night.

Each of us felt so blessed to have one more Christmas with Scott. We continued to believe that there would be a miracle.

Happy Birthday, Denny

Christmas break from school was rapidly ending. It was hard to believe that I had spent almost the entire month of December with my family, watching over my baby brother. Scott's white cell count was finally starting to increase which meant that his immune system was kicking into gear. He was starting to get some of his strength back. Scott had received more than 74 pints of blood, packed cells, and platelets and he had finally stopped hemorrhaging. He had not needed any more transfusions for several days. Scott's lungs and kidneys were still not working properly, but the doctors had told us that they felt Scott had turned a corner and that he was improving.

> Scott had received **more than 74 pints** of blood, packed cells, and platelets

It was at that point that I decided to head back to Virginia. We said our goodbyes, feeling more hopeful than any of us had felt in weeks. As I stepped into the elevator, the head oncologist on Scott's team of doctors followed me in. When he turned around and looked at me, I told him, "I am leaving but I expect you to take the very best care of my brother and to not let anything else happen to him!" The oncologist assured me that he would look after Scott as if he were his own son. The plan, he told me, was to let Scott rest for a couple days. On the 30th, they would take him off the ventilator and put in a trachea tube in order to allow him more freedom to move. The medical team also hoped that this procedure would help reduce the constant agitation that Scott had been experiencing since he had been on the ventilator.

My oldest brother, Denny and his wife planned to stay with my parents. Mike, his wife and I left on December 28th. I flew back to Virginia on December 29th.

I had barely been home twenty-four hours when the phone rang. It was Mother and, after I said, "Hello," she said, "Jo, I wanted to let you know that Scott passed away this morning."

"What had she said? How could that be? I was confused and frightened. Just a couple days ago, they had said he was getting better, turned the corner. They were removing him from the ventilator! Liars!"

At that moment, I hated every one of those arrogant, condescending, medical professionals in white coats. I could tell my mom was in shock so I asked to speak with Denny. That day was his 35th birthday. Denny got on the line and told me that, as the family had left the night before, they were told by the night nurses, to be back in the morning by 9:00 am, if they wanted to see Scott before his tracheotomy which was considered to be a minor procedure. The medical staff had planned to remove Scott from the ventilator and put in a trachea tube.

Instead of waiting for my parents to arrive, the hospital called them very early that morning and asked them to come immediately. When Mom and Dad arrived, a chaplain met them and announced that Scott had passed away a few minutes prior to their arrival. There was not a cowardly doctor or nurse in sight.

At first, my parents were confused and did not really comprehend the chaplain's words. They were in shock. The chaplain first asked if they wanted to see Scott and, then, inferred that his dying was probably a blessing. But, he caught himself, and never finished the sentence.

Jo Hamilton

My family went into Scott's room and there he was, finally at peace. No more fighting—the restraints, the ventilator, or death. The EET, or breathing tube, was still in place. A doctor eventually came into the room and explained to the family that, when the nurse had checked on Scott in the early morning hours, she discovered a hole in the PEEP tubing running from the ventilator to the tube in his mouth that directly fed oxygen into his lungs.

This was a big deal because Scott's lung tissue was heavily scarred from the high oxygen content they had been giving him during prior weeks. This leak would have immediately compromised his oxygen level. The night shift staff made the decision to do nothing at the time since Scott was scheduled to have the ventilator removed later in the morning.

This decision had been the final blow to Scott's already threatened respiratory system. By the time the shift changed, Scott's condition had become an emergency. He had become so cyanotic from no longer maintaining proper oxygen levels, the lack of enough oxygen was affecting not only his breathing but, also, his heartbeat. Scott was then rushed STAT to the operating room. His minor procedure had turned into a major catastrophe.

No one could explain how Scott had managed to survive so long after such an enormous cisplatin overdose, only to be suffocated to death by another completely preventable mistake, at the very hands of the professionals he had so completely trusted with his life.

It was almost unbearable to think of Scott paralyzed with drugs and restraints, silenced by the ventilator tube, unable to cry out for help. There was nothing else for him to do but die.

Instead of letting Scott rest in peace, there was one more thing the hospital wanted from him. My mother explained that they were planning on going back to Iowa right away but the hospital wanted to perform an autopsy. If my parents agreed to the autopsy, the hospital would not release Scott's body for a few more days. My parents felt that they had already given them their youngest child yet, in the end, the doctors persuaded them to go against their instincts once again and leave Scott there for the autopsy. No doubt, they had to collect more of their precious data for the study in which Scott had unselfishly agreed to participate.

Even after his death, my parents honored Scott's end of the agreement.

For The Love of Scott!

To Scott
12-30-1983

He was of my flesh and of my blood
The same fair-haired, blue-eyed boy
That mom laid in my arms on his fourth day of life.

We spent so much of our time together those first few months,
I couldn't let him out of my sight.
The hours we spent in "Grandma's old rocker."
He only watching-and me having the
conversations of my life with him!
Oh how he listened..
Oh how he watched...
God, how I came to love him!!

The years were so precious and
only moments compared to forever...
Our time together grew to be less and less,
But our bond of love grew stronger and stronger.

Time and miles came between us,
as our lives took different paths,
But, the love never faltered and we both knew that what we shared was
far more important than how often we shared it.

Jo Hamilton

For The Love of Scott!

The last time I talked with him, he still
Seemed like the little babe I used to hold,
only even more helpless...and there was nothing
I could do to keep him safe and alive...
All the love I had for him could not take his pain away.

Where have you gone, Scottie boy?
I watched as you died before my very eyes,
and I could no longer see because of the tears.

Four times they injected life back into your human pump. Many more
times we said our good-byes to you and hoped every time we were wrong.
They ate up your malignancy with their wonder drug and your strong,
young body with it.

You are a hero, my little soldier.
You showed them what you were made of and
you didn't give up easily.
If you were talking with me now,
you'd tell me you were in a better place and not to cry for you.

But I have to say to you Scott, letting go is very hard for us who are still
living and very painful.
I miss you so and maybe I am not as strong as you.
I am not going to tell you goodbye....
Just to wait for me, and we will talk again.....
at a better time and place, for eternity.

Jo Hamilton

Home, Where the Tall Corn Grows

Scott's body was finally returned home to Iowa in January of 1984. That winter had turned even more bitter and cold. We had to wait to have Scott's funeral because the ground was frozen so hard that the groundskeeper at the cemetery was unable to dig the grave.

The funeral was like nothing I would have imagined. I had expected a quiet, peaceful, dignified service for our community and relatives to say, "Goodbye," to our youngest family member. Due to the religious beliefs of the Catholic Church, our family had to observe three different wakes, or viewings, along with a rite called, "Praying of the Rosary."

Before the first viewing, our family discussed the option of having a closed-casket service. As Scott's brothers and sister, we felt that his physical appearance was so unnatural that it would be too emotional for his friends and extended family to witness an open casket. We pleaded with our parents. We knew that Scott would have hated for his friends to see him this way but our mother was adamant that the casket be left opened.

We all watched Mom as she gently and lovingly attempted to comb Scott's wig the way he had worn his hair but it just was not working. No amount of make-up could camouflage Scott's discolored skin, caused by the vast amount of chemicals in his lifeless body. Thankfully, the funeral director suggested a compromise. He placed a thin, patterned, black veil over the casket to help mask the traumatizing image.

Despite the funeral director's best efforts, the shock could be seen in the eyes of Scott's friends. They were horrified and grief-stricken.

I watched as many of Scott's friends entered the funeral home, shocked and bewildered by what they were seeing and experiencing. Most of his college friends had assumed that, after their summer break, they would all be together again in the fall, celebrating their senior year before heading out to fulfill their destinies. Scott's decision not to share his illness with any of them only deepened their confusion. When friends approached his casket shaken and crying, some fell to their knees in disbelief. Scott looked nothing like the young man they had seen that spring. The body in the casket was a shadow of the strong athlete that they had known in college.

"What happened to our buddy? How could he be dead? He wasn't even sick!" some of them must have thought. Many of their questions were never answered and, perhaps, the saddest part of all was that they never had the opportunity to say goodbye to their friend.

Before leaving the funeral home and in route to the church for the final mass, I watched as my family said their last goodbyes to Scott.

My mother stared into the casket at the body of her youngest child, her baby. She never spoke a word nor shed a tear. She was overwhelmed with grief. It was almost as though she was still trying to comprehend what had happened or, perhaps, she was wishing that Scott would wake up just one more time.

My father was inconsolable. Sobbing out of control, he draped himself across the casket and kept repeating, "Scott, oh, Scott." None of us were equipped to help him with his profound loss. His youngest son was dead at age 23 along with one of Dad's dreams, to watch Scott play ball in the major leagues.

My oldest brother, Denny, who was typically cool, calm, and steady, collapsed into his wife's arms. They hung onto each other for support as they cried together.

Mike, the sensitive child in our family, leaned into the casket and softly whispered something to Scott and, then, broke into tears.

I had said my goodbyes to my baby brother so many times during the past month that I felt empty and incapable of saying another. I turned away, feeling the most isolated and lonely that I had ever felt in my entire life.

After the viewings and before the funeral mass, it is customary in the Catholic Church to close the casket.

The winter of 1983 went down in the record books as one of the coldest and most brutal winters in Iowa history. I can attest to that. It was the winter when the hearts of our family were frozen with grief.

The Other Scott

Even though we had laid to rest, our Scott Hamilton in the little cemetery of our small, rural, Iowa community, our family continued to watch Scott Hamilton, the figure skater, go on to win Olympic Gold in the Winter Games of 1984. His name was in the press frequently throughout the 1980s. In 1984, this Scott turned professional and created, *Scott Hamilton's American Tour*, which later became known as, *Stars on Ice*.

This Scott continued to perform with *Stars on Ice* and co-produced the show for fifteen more years before he retired from the tour in 2001. He has since returned and is producing new shows again. This Scott has been a skating commentator for many years, beginning in 1985, and he currently serves on the Board of Directors for the Special Olympics International. He was inducted into the United States Olympic Hall of Fame in 1990.

When the skater, Scott Hamilton, was diagnosed with testicular cancer in 1990 and treated at a renowned hospital in the Midwest, the parallels with our beloved Scott were rekindled. He continued to skate after his chemo treatments but, on November 12, 2004, it was announced that Scott had been diagnosed with a benign brain tumor. He was successfully treated at the same hospital that had treated his testicular cancer. Scott had another occurrence in 2011. Thirteen years to the day of his testicular cancer surgery, he was again successfully operated on to treat the brain tumor. It was reported that, due to a nicked optical artery, there were some complications during the surgery and Scott was left with impaired vision in his right eye.

Despite these challenges, Scott Hamilton continues to be an inspirational role model to thousands of fans, kids, and families. Every time he has fought back from the difficulties that life has dealt him and continues to live his life with passion, strength, and love, I am reminded of my little brother, Scott, and the spirit he carried until the moment of his death. It will forever make me wonder what might have been.

Afterward

Almost three decades have passed since Scott's death.
Each of us has lived a lifetime without him. His death
affected everyone in my family in a profoundly different
way. Our memories have faded and we all recall things a
little bit differently. This story has been written from my
observations, remembrances, and feelings of the
experiences and events that happened those many years
ago.

As one might imagine, the toll it took on my parents as
a couple and as Scott's guardians was unimaginable. To say
that the first few years after Scott's death were rough on
them is an understatement. It was easy for Denny, Mike,
and I, as the surviving children, to understand why the
divorce rate is so high among couples that lose a child. It
was our observation that our parents had stopped
communicating with each other and, when they did, their
exchanges were angry and sharp. None of us knew how to
handle this behavior in our parents but we knew that it had
little to do with them and everything to do with losing their

son, their baby. There was no way for any of us to comprehend the depth of our parent's pain. Several years after Scott's passing, my father shared his theory on Scott's overdose with me. It is his belief the hospital discovered the overdose several days before they shared it with us. He thinks the hospital dismissed Scott, believing he would quickly die, perhaps even on the trip back to Iowa and that would be the end of the story. They did not count on Scott's strength, his resilience, his heart, or his family bond to keep his love for life alive. Of course, we will never know the truth behind this theory, and it does not really matter. Maybe Scott did not beat the odds, but he gave them all something to think about for the rest of their days on this earth.

My brother, Denny, kept most of his emotions bottled up inside. It was only during 2010 when I started to write Scott's story, that we really spoke in detail about the day that Scott died and what it had been like for him and his family. Denny shared with me how our parents had reacted when they were told of Scott's death. He also told me about an event that happened at a restaurant within hours after Scott's passing.

For The Love of Scott!

Mom and Dad, Denny and his wife were seated and waiting for the server when Denny and Lynn saw a young man who looked so much like our little brother, Scott, that they could have been twins. He passed right by their table, looked directly at them and said, "Hi, how ya' doing?"

Denny told me that he looked at his wife and she looked at him. They could barely breathe, they were so stunned. He said he was so drawn to the young man that he got up from the table and followed the same path that the young man had taken toward the kitchen. By the time Denny reached the doorway, the young man had disappeared. Denny approached several employees who were within close proximity but no one knew anything about the young man he was asking about. In fact, they said that there were no men scheduled to work that day. Our parents never saw this young man.

My nephew, Chad, Denny's youngest child, was very young when Scott died and asked us many questions on the ride to the cemetery the day of Scott's funeral. "Where did Uncle Scott go? Am I going to die, too? Is he going to come home? Am I going to get sick?" For years, Chad suffered from separation anxiety every time his parents went away for a few hours, in fear that they would not come home again. Every time he came down with an illness, Chad would always ask if he was going to die, "like Uncle Scott."

Years later, Denny's oldest daughter, Robyn, was in the kitchen working while her daughter, Madie, who was about three years old at the time, was in the next room alone playing. Robyn began listening to Madie having a conversation with someone. She was laughing and joyfully dancing around in her playroom. Robyn walked in and asked Madie who she was talking to and the little girl said, "Scott, I'm talking to Scott."

Robyn had been in grade school when Scott had died and as far as she could remember, she had never mentioned Scott's name around her daughter. Madie was heard speaking to Scott again within that same year.

Denny's sharing of these stories with me was a gift. I would never have known about them had I not kept my promise to tell Scott's story.

My brother, Mike, the closest in age to Scott, had fallen into a deep depression after the death. He told me later that, in those first few months after Scott's passing, he had wished that he would have been taken instead of Scott. Mike's faith was challenged and we all witnessed the ways in which this loss of faith affected other relationships in his life. To this day, we all have issues with doctors and hospitals.

A few years ago before a Thanksgiving dinner, we were all gathered in the kitchen talking when Dad told us that he had been dreaming about Scott a few nights before. Dad said that he woke and sat straight up. "There, at the foot of the bed, was Scott, standing and looking at me. When I reached out my hand to touch him, Scott smiled and disappeared."

Of course, someone then asked Dad, "Are you sure you were awake?"

Dad answered, "Yes, I was very much awake."

I witnessed my parents slowly begin to reconnect with each other and eventually engage in life again, though in a different way. Their lives would never again hold the same meaning or level of passion for them. For Dad, seeing a baseball diamond will always be bittersweet.

In April, 1984, four months after Scotts' death, there was a warm dampness in the air, the type that stirs your senses awake. I was on my way home from work. Everything was on the cusp of bursting open with new life. I took in a deep breath and held it for a few moments before exhaling. Feeling a twinge of joy, I suddenly remembered that Scott was gone and that I would not see him this spring or summer or fall or winter or, ever.

Instantly, I plunged into a dark place of grief, thinking that death would be a welcome end if it would mean seeing my baby brother again.

For The Love of Scott!

Marking Time
3-1-1984

Sometimes it's ok, but it never seems to be all right.
There are times when feeling finds its way into my senses--
by mistake and I glaze it over with
the thickest wall I can build......

Maybe it will all end soon, and
maybe it will never be over......
All I can be sure of for, now is how empty I feel . . .
and that is my reality.
Will there ever be anything else?

Jo Hamilton

This kind of sorrow plagued me for years. I stopped going to church and spent long periods of time alone. I terminated relationship after relationship, quickly and without explanation, trusting no one. I lost complete faith in the medical profession and changed careers. Then, one day, I was tired of feeling dead inside and decided to enter grief therapy. That process lasted three long years. Besides watching my little brother die, this therapy was the hardest, most painful thing I have ever done. Thanks to an extraordinary therapist, my best friend and a little black poodle named Cher, I found a way to push the shade back up and let in the light.

I hung on to the words my friend would say to me daily, "I know you may not believe me right now but, one day, you are going to feel better, I promise."

On some level, I must have believed those words because I did not check out of life, even though there were many days that I wanted to do just that. Then, suddenly, the day came. One morning shortly after waking up, I felt joy in my heart again and knew that I wanted to be back among the living, to have meaning and passion in my life again.

My broken heart was healing and I could finally rejoice in happier memories of Scott.

There were still many questions that I needed to seek out answers for and, in doing so, my path lead me to hospice. I knew that becoming a volunteer would be a key piece in helping me to heal. Not everything in me would be fixed, of course. Even today, there is a certain kind of anxiety that comes if any loved one or I go to the doctor. I quiz my family members and friends to the extreme about any medical procedures, medications, or hospitalizations they are having, are taking, or going to have. The experience of the medical harm done to Scott has been permanently recorded in my family's cellular memory, changing who we might have been and who we eventually became.

Because of Scott's experience, things in life continue to manifest themselves in unexpected ways.

What Can You Do to Stay Safe?

Before beginning this book, I was eager to do research in order to see any wonderful progress that had been made towards quality care in the medical profession, specifically concerning medication errors. If I had found amazing results and statistics, I may have never completed the promise that I had made to my little brother.

One night, shortly after I began writing his story and wondering if I would finally be able to complete it, I asked Scott for help through contemplation. I had called on him many times throughout this process and he had always come through for me.

I was watching the Discovery channel that night when a broadcast entitled, *Chasing Zero: Winning the War on Health Care Harm* began playing. Actor, Dennis Quaid, produced the movie and Care Fusion, Association of Community Organizations for Reform Now (ACORN), and The Texas Medical Institute of Technology (TMIT) funded and supported the documentary. Immediately, I hit the record button. "Thank you little brother!" I said aloud.

For The Love of Scott!

Dennis Quaid had a personal, stake in this film. In 2007, the hospital nursing staff when given their blood thinner medication shortly after their birth overdosed his infant twins by 1,000 times. This error was attributed to a misreading of the label on the bottle that was similar to the label on another bottle of the same medication, only with a different dosage. The nurses simply did not pay attention to the dosage or the slight color difference on the two labels, before injecting it into BOTH of his babies.

Quaid and his wife learned through their experience that this type of error happens all too frequently and usually with fatal results. His family's outcome had a happy ending and today, his twins are alive, well, and thriving. Obviously, this experience changed his family forever. The entire article, written by Meg Grant, can be found in the October 2010 issue AARP Magazine, pages 46-49 and pages 77-79.

Quaid became an activist championing change in the health care profession. He spoke in front of the National Press Club and Members of Congress on Capitol Hill, advocating for reform that would help stop the careless and needless deaths that are occurring everyday across the

Jo Hamilton

country in numerous healthcare facilities. It does not matter
if the medical facilities are the most prestigious and well-
funded in the world or the smallest rural county hospital.
None of them are immune to making fatal, preventable
mistakes that take the lives of the people who we know and
love.

It was while watching the documentary that I learned
almost every answer to the questions that I needed to know
about our present day health care field. We, as consumers,
patients, and advocates, have a false sense of security.

I recommend that everyone watch this documentary.
The information will increase your chances and the chances
for those you love of surviving a medical crisis. This
program could literally save your life and the lives of those
you love. TMIT is distributing the DVD free of charge to
every hospital in the country. At the time of the publishing
of this book, the first in the series, *Chasing Zero: Winning
the War on Healthcare Harm* is still available as a free
download from TMIT's website, www.safetyleaders.org.
The program tells the stories of medical-error victims as
well as listing those providers who have made mistakes.
You can also send for the free DVD. The site offers free

classes and surveys, as well as online webinars, for registered users.

Would our Scott have survived the overdose if he had not suffocated to death in the end? It is doubtful. Everything I have researched to date tells us that, although there have been incidents where survival has occurred, no one given more than 300 mgs., total dosage, of cisplatin is alive today. Scott received over 800 mgs total. If the overdose is caught within 24-48 hours and the protocol administered immediately, the chances of surviving dramatically increase.

As of the beginning of 2011, I could find no published guidelines or antidote for counteracting this type of toxicity, although research is ongoing. It is purely through trial and error that medical mistakes are addressed. Cisplatin is a tremendously potent, toxic drug and is widely used in the field of oncology. Its use in the non-specific targeting of cancer cells commonly results in adverse effects and toxicity affecting almost every body system. While watching *Chasing Zero*, it was horrifying to learn that, since 1999 to present day, 100,000 people still die every year because of harm received during health care.

Jo Hamilton

Other reports state that the number could be as high as 30,000 a month! I recently read an article in *Consumer Report* magazine by the CR President, Jim Guest, which stated that a more accurate statistic is, "Nine million Americans a year are being harmed by medical care errors." It further comments that this data reflects only the errors that we know about. In 2003, Consumer Union, the non-profit publisher of *Consumer Report*, launched a campaign to make hospital infection rates available to the consumer. The annual infections acquired by patients while in a hospital environment is 200,000 cases, easily. This statistic is alarming not just because of the loss of life but, also, because of the billions of dollars in health care costs that are incurred (May 2011, pp 6-7).

Consumer Union has since helped pass laws in 27 states and in Washington, D.C., that require public reporting of infection occurrences. During 2011, hospitals nationwide will have similar requirements. Very soon, it is reported, Medicare will link hospital payments to the rate of infections.

Public reports are putting more pressure on hospitals to decrease their infection rates. In 2011, President Obama announced that a federal initiative to reduce infections and limit the high cost of readmissions was in the works. However, infections are not the only problem. It has been reported that 25 % of patients are harmed by the hospital care that they receive. To date, there are no state or federal laws or mandates that require health care facilities to report ANY of their mistakes or errors resulting in injury, harm, or death to their patients. There is a newly formed project called *The Safe Patient Project* that pressures states to make hospitals disclose drug and surgical errors. This project also proposes that patients, as consumers, should also have access to complaints and actions against doctors just as there is with any other consumer services.

There are other factors contributing to the making of medical errors. For example, the way that doctors write their prescriptions for chemotherapy treatment, there is no standard verbiage used. Some write the word, "sessions," and some use, "series," or, "cycles." The interpretation is not clear. Is a session one day or one week? Does a cycle consist of one 24-hour period or the entire length of treatment? The lack of standard word usage is very confusing to both the pharmacists and health care staff. A

Jo Hamilton

doctor's handwriting has been and continues to be a well-known factor for errors. Hospitals and clinics are presently moving towards instituting a digital ordering system that will certainly have a positive effect on addressing errors caused by a doctor's bad handwriting.

Dr. Charles Denham, Chairperson of TMIT, believes that it is possible to bring the 25 % statistic regarding medical errors to almost 0 and, 0 is the target number.

Dr. Denham is working with a team of doctors, including one from the Mayo Clinic. Dr. Stephen Swenson MD, MMM, is the director for an organization called Quality Mayo Clinic. This organization sends out surveys to numerous health care providers. One of the questions the survey asks the providers to rate is their quality of care. The results from one survey showed that fewer than half of the boards from these institutions even rated *quality of care* as a priority in their facility!

The documentary, *Chasing Zero*, lists numerous agencies and organizations that are working on making improvements in the health care field. The Institute for Health Care Improvement (IHI), the National Quality

Forum (NQF), and the Agency for Health Care Research & Quality are a few listed.

These agencies have tabulated the research data and made numerous suggestions and guidelines to improve the quality and care of patients. They have provided guidelines and checklists for hospital personnel that can help personnel be more accountable and accurate in their care of patients. The goal is to eliminate common errors that occur due to the repetitiveness in their jobs.

The World Health Organization is working to break through the wall of silence that exists among the staff in health facilities that tend to protect each other. If a doctor or nurse plays a role in the death of a patient, no matter how careless or blatant it may be, the death is termed "wrongful death." They are exempt from being charged with murder or killing unless a court of law proves differently, which is rarely the case. Many hospitals are self-insured. They can play a very long waiting game when it comes to settling a malpractice case. Most medical errors ARE accidents. The problem when a harmful error occurs, the barriers immediately go into place. The first barrier begins with fear. The health care provider is afraid of punishment of termination and as a result, may lie, not communicate at all, or hide. So the very people, whose input is critically needed determine how to stop the problem from reoccurring, are alienated from the solution. Ultimately, the hospitals need to take responsibility for the problem by using all of their resources to come up with a solution to fix it.

According to the National Quality Forum (NQF) statistics, nearly 15 million instances of medical harm occur each year. The costs associated with medical harm have been estimated to be between $17 billion to $29 billion per year in expenses, lost productivity, lost income and disability and, in far too many cases, death. **That is $17,000,000,000** to **$29,000,000,000.**

The question in my mind is, "Would any of these protocols or guidelines have made a difference in Scott's outcome?" We will never know. It is a mammoth undertaking. One of the largest obstacles is getting all of the different medical systems to communicate with each other. The date entry still has to be manually input and once again, we are relying on the accuracy of human beings to get it right.

For The Love of Scott!

A few weeks ago, I was having a discussion with a good friend, who is a retired Navy nurse. We were talking about Scott's story and she said to me, "If this had happened today, Scott would probably still be alive." With further explanation she stated that presently, when a pharmacy deals with a lethal or controlled substance, two pharmacists must check each other. Both have to sign off that the order has been filled accurately.

There is also a system in place for the facilities that dispense medication. If the order calls for X dosage of medication and the pharmacist requests a different or higher dosage, the system should electronically send an alert asking, "Are you sure you want X dosage? This is out of normal parameters!" The pharmacist has the final option of overriding the system if he chooses so.

The final checkpoint lies with the nurses and doctors that check the medication in and then check it out and administer it to the patient. At least two nurses have to check that the dosage is correct for the assigned patient and then sign the chart, noting that it is accurate.

As you can clearly see, even though there are numerous checks and balances all along the way, just as there were

Jo Hamilton

with Scotts' medication, there are several places where the system still needs and relies on a human being to do the right thing. Perhaps Scott's death was a catalyst to the creation of some of these guidelines.

The human element is still the most unpredictable part of the equation and will always be a factor in health care treatment. We must determine a way to include the human factor in the part of the equation that strives to improve and perfect the process. I pray that day is closer than we think!!

What can we do to keep ourselves and our loved ones safe? Find your local Discovery Channel or go online and check the schedule for *Chasing Zero: Winning the War on Healthcare Reform*. It can also be viewed online or obtained free from Discovery. Part 2 of the series came out before the completion of this book.

The producers list a complete selection of Continuing Medical Education (CMEs) courses. Part 2 shows numerous changes that are already taking place and have made a difference. Several large hospitals, including Mayo Clinic and Cleveland Clinic have already adopted the *Green Light Approach* and are implementing safe practices.

The problem that still remains is that safe practices are still voluntary. Someday soon it must become mandatory.

If you are a parent of young boys, especially around the age of 15, educate them about self-examines. According to ehealthMD website, testicular cancer usually strikes men between the ages of 15 and 35, and is one of the most common cancers in men of this age group. Male seniors however, are not immune to the disease. That said, this type of cancer is rare: it accounts for only about 1 % of all cancers in men. It is more common in Caucasian men than in other ethnic groups. As with most things, the earlier the detection, the better. Most testicular cancers are found by individuals or their partners and they are found by accident or when doing a self-examination. The cure rate statistics are above 90 % if discovered and treated early. Even advanced testicular cancer has a 70 % cure rate.

If you are diagnosed with a life threatening or terminal illness or need hospitalization, designate a friend or family member who can be with you to help monitor your care, especially at night, on holidays, and weekends.

Be persistent. Insist that doctors and nurses identify you when they come into your room, say your name, check your identification wristband, and match it to your chart. Make sure hospital personnel wash their hands before administering your medications, removing your catheter, changing your wound dressings, and checking or marking a surgical site. Note all medications you are given. If any seem unfamiliar, ask the nurse its purpose. If anything seems unusual or out of the norm for you or your body, tell your caretaker and make them check and recheck your medication, the dosage, and the side effects.

Be vigilant and forceful. You may get resistance from all sides—TRUST YOUR INTUITION—it could save your life!

The Lessons Learned

As I grow older, I have become much more philosophical about life and death. After much meditation and prayer, I was finally able to open my heart again. I have forgiven and let go of the anger, guilt, and cynicism that had invaded my soul. After returning to the medical profession that I had loved so much, I began doing what I had been doing for most of my life, assisting others in the process of living and dying. Scott's life had a purpose, as we all do in this world. His journey included a horrendous, slow, and painful death. For those personnel in that medical facility who attended to Scott and was touched by his experience, my hope is that one of the many lessons they learned has been that they became better caretakers and paid closer attention when administering lethal medications.

Maybe one day, a pre-med, nursing student, or resident physician, whose medical experiences and compassion, has not yet gained equal ground with their arrogance, attitude, and ego, will hear about Scott's story and it will change their thought process or focus. Perhaps a professor teaching a class in pharmaceuticals or bedside manner will pick up this book, read Scott's story and it will affect their students in a profound, positive, and permanent way.

What have we, his family, learned? It has obviously been different for each one of us but, for me, Scott's experience has taught me much: everlasting love, trusting my inner voice and intuition, finding my strength, becoming a strong, persistent, and unyielding advocate for my care and for those I love. Maybe the most important lesson of all is forgiveness.

Jo Hamilton

My dad once said to me, "If it had been the disease that had killed him, I could have accepted it, but it was the people. The people he trusted more than anything with his life. That is what I have the hardest time with." I think Dad's statement truly echoes the feelings of our entire family. I cannot forget the roles that the people played in this but it is really the system that is broken and that is what we need to fix more than anything. With all the wonderful advances in modern technology today, humans are still fallible and that may be our biggest challenge.

Scott Hamilton Memorial Score Board

After Scotts' death, our family received more than $3,000 in memorial gifts, as well as several Mass cards and flowers, from our small farm community.

For The Love of Scott!

Because of Scott's love for the game of baseball, we used the money to purchase a new electronic baseball scoreboard for the high school baseball field. The words "Scott Hamilton Memorial" will forever be displayed at the top of the scoreboard. The ball diamond is right across the street from my parents' house, an easy view for them through the large picture window where they can watch ball games anytime, day, or night.

This book, *For the Love of Scott!*, has been my baby brother's story. Writing it has been a difficult labor of love, emotionally hard to recount at times. I am sorry that it has taken me 27 years to do the writing, but as it turns out, the timing is just perfect. It brought me back into the memories of how strong Scott's heart, courage and strength were, especially throughout the last month of his life. It is especially startling how much my family and I still miss him. There are times when I find myself wondering what Scott would have looked like at 50 years of age, how many nieces, nephews or grandkids he would have given to us and what kind of person would he have grown up to be?

A few months ago, a very special woman from Scott's past who became a wonderful and competent nurse, wrote to me on Facebook and asked if Scott was once in a band named, "The Fulton Street Band."

My dear little brother Scott,

Do you know, that after almost 30 years, there are people outside of your family, here on this earth, that still remember your name, your twinkling blue eyes, your wonderful smile, your long skinny legs and big feet and that you played in a rock and roll band? I know this must make you smile! You may never have made it to the big leagues, little brother, but you will be remembered for something much bigger than baseball . . . and it has already happened.

Your sister,

Jo

Scott Alan Joseph Hamilton
September 22, 1960 – December 30, 1983

Jo Hamilton

Expressions of Gratitude

My gratitude, to the many persons that helped and encouraged me to write Scott's story and enabled me to keep the promise, is beyond measure.

I must first thank my family, both immediate and extended, for their patience, their strength; their belief and their support. They have helped me in ways they will never know, throughout my entire life. I know that taking this walk with me again was painfully necessary and I thank all of you from the bottom of my heart!

Donna-thank you for all your love, support, vision, and encouragement throughout this process --from the very beginning to the very end and especially for "Ms. Mac"---that really showed me, I could finally write a book! Thank You, Thank You, Thank You!

Pauline-thank you for believing in my gifts and talent long before I even knew I had them. Thanks for my ever present "Iowa" buddy, Dodger, who was my comfort and joy throughout this entire emotional process. Thank You!

Suzanne-thank you for knowing this book would be born, long before I did, and for planting the seed in my head and my heart those many years ago. Thank you for all the hours you spent sharing your wisdom, opinions, editing, advice, and most of all your enduring friendship. Thank You!

Jeane H-You, more than anyone, showed me how to open my heart again and I will forever be grateful. I thank you for showing me a new path to follow which led me back to love. Thank You!

Constance-Thank you for living in Asheville and sharing your exuberant personality, beautiful art, and lovely garden-especially your favorite flower! You helped me to rekindle my dream, you inspired me again, and somehow lit the spark that needed to be reignited. Thank You!

Brenda-Thank you for being such a wonderful friend for all these years and the best cheerleader EVER! Your love, support, advice, encouragement, and feedback have been priceless! Thank You!

For The Love of Scott!

Dody-Thank you for coming back into my life when I needed it the most. I still believe you are an Angel! I thank you for your editing talents, your joy of living, your wisdom and support and your long and lasting friendship. It is so good to have found on way back into each other's lives! Thank You!

Maggie-Thank you for coming to my rescue when I called on you! Thank you for loving my brother even though you never had the chance to meet him. I am grateful for the many talents and abilities you have shared with my family. I knew the moment I met you that you were a keeper, and I was right! Thank You

I also want to thank the thousands of health care professionals who go to work every day with their best intentions —to do no harm. They work in an environment that is stressful, painful, unforgiving, and emotionally draining. They are underpaid and overworked. They work with their hearts on their sleeves because they care deeply about all of it; the patient, their families, the outcome. I still love the medical field and my constant prayer is that things keep getting better and better for everyone involved. I believe with all my heart that it will, and one day we will be able to reach that new statistic—ZERO!

A Percentage of the proceeds from this book will be dedicated to The Scott Hamilton CARES Initiative. This program supports and promotes world-class research and quality care that may one day lead to a cure for cancer. The goal is to empower patients and their families through education and guidance while taking the walk through cancer treatments and survivorship.

Author

Jo Hamilton, born on an Iowa farm in the heartland of America, while in junior high school, published her first short story in the national magazine, "The Student Writer," and received a cash award. As an adult, one of her poems was selected for publication in the poetry book "Sunspots," by Palomar. She was also presented "The Golden Poet Award for 1989" in Washington DC by Bob Hope, Helen Hayes, and Willard Scott for the poem "His House."

Jo attended school in Minnesota for medical technology. She worked in traditional Western medicine, as a teacher and health care worker, for 27 years. Following the tragic family crisis described in "For the Love of Scott!" by Olmstead Publishing, Jo left the medical field angry, bitter, and disillusioned.

Because of this situation, Jo investigated alternative modalities and began writing a new chapter in her own life. She studied the power of energetic healing touch, becoming a Reiki Master Teacher. Jo's path led her to work as an acute care hospice volunteer. In 2000, Jo became a Licensed Massage Therapist. Besides therapeutic massage, her private practice includes aromatherapy, cranial sacral therapy, reflexology, Reiki, and Raindrop Therapy Technique. Jo also teaches Reiki and meditation classes.

Literary Works:

1964-Short Story--"Because of a Doll"-The Student Writer 2/1964-nationally published-monthly magazine published by the Academy Publishing Corporation-Fort Lauderdale, Florida
1971- Poem-"I Suppose"-Sunspots-Collection of Contemporary Original Poetry-published by Palomar Publishing Company-Ca.(2/1971)
1979- Poem- "Forever At Least"-Best Loved Contemporary Poems-2/1979-World of Poetry Press-Sacramento, Ca.(2/1979)
1981-Poem- "It's Easy"-The World's Great Contemporary Poems-World of Poetry Press-Sacramento, Ca.(2/1981)
1989-Poem-"His House"-The World Treasury of Great Poems Vol. III World of Poetry Press-Sacramento, CA (2/1989)

Made in the USA
Charleston, SC
02 October 2011